SURVIVING THE PARAPHRASE

Other books by Frank Davey

Poetry

D-Day and After
City of the Gulls and Sea
Bridge Force
The Scarred Hull
Four Myths for Sam Perry
Weeds
Griffon
King of Swords
l'An Trentiesme: Selected Poems
Arcana
The Clallam
War Poems
Capitalistic Affection!
The Arches: Selected Poems
The Louis Riel Organ & Piano Company

Criticism

Earle Birney
Louis Dudek and Raymond Souster
From There to Here
Margaret Atwood: a Feminist Poetics

Editor

Tish, No. 1-19

Frank Davey

SURVIVING THE PARAPHRASE

Eleven Essays on Canadian Literature

with a Preface by Eli Mandel

Turnstone Press

Turnstone Press Limited
603-99 King Street
Winnipeg, Manitoba
Canada R3B 1H7

Second Printing, 1986.

This book was typeset by B/W Type Service Ltd. and printed at Hignell Printing Ltd. for Turnstone Press. Published with the assistance of the Manitoba Arts Council and the Canada Council.

Printed and bound in Canada.

Acknowledgements: Some of these essays were first published in *Canadian Literature, Open Letter,* and *Studies in Canadian Literature.*

for Linda

CONTENTS

PREFACE

From its earliest beginnings, Canadian criticism has been a surprisingly aggressive art, its practitioners calling on their skills of polemic and contention. As editor of *Tish* magazine in the sixties, the young Frank Davey certainly contributed to this reputation. His colleague and fellow poet, George Bowering, writes of him with respect to that period, "He has a history of confrontation with poets and critics over poetics and *belief*." And nothing in the present volume is likely to alter the view that he is often an antithetical writer, defining his views in the negative by a kind of dialectical process. It is intriguing to notice that he develops the impressive poetics and critical theory of this volume not by articulating views he espouses but by clarifying and consolidating the error about him. So he begins with an important exposé of the direction Canadian criticism has taken from the fifties to the seventies, his startling attack on thematic criticism in 1974, and follows with a brilliant series of essays on the language, imagery, form, and themes of writers with whom he is often not at all in sympathy. It is as if he is clearing the way for a poetics that yet remains to take its own shape and form.

Still, "antithetical" is not quite the right word to describe Frank Davey's criticism, nor does it tell the whole story of his achievement. The essays collected here have been written against the background of Davey's long and close intellectual engagement with the major critical issues of his day. His work includes two major studies of important contemporary writers, *Earle Birney* and *Dudek and Souster*, and his invaluable, perhaps indispensible, guide to the work of sixty English Canadian writers, *From There to Here*, a volume that with Davey's introduction and precise essays on the work of significant contemporary poets and novelists, maps out the shift from modern to post-modernist techniques in Canadian writing. As well during this period, Davey has continued to edit the influential magazine of studies in post-modernist issues and writers, *Open Letter*. To add to this body of work, this collection of incidental essays provides a clear sense of his very substantial contribution to contemporary criticism in Canada.

That contribution here takes three special forms: 1) assessments of the position criticism in Canada has developed theoretically and in practice, 2) individual studies of the direction and character of the work of particular individuals in prose and poetry, and 3) theoretical studies of contemporary techniques and concerns in writing. The first is without question the most spectacular aspect of these essays. Davey's essay "Surviving the Paraphrase" is a classic of its kind, bold, forthright, uncompromising. It advances the view that an inadequate critical theory has dominated Canadian criticism through the period to the mid 1970's and it sketches alternative approaches. It attacks the so-called thematic criticism deployed by certain followers of Northrop Frye, notably Margaret Atwood and D. G. Jones, and offers other critical possibilities: phenomenological criticism, genre studies, linguistic analysis, regional concerns. In all this, Davey is acutely prophetic of the direction Canadian studies has in fact taken. But more importantly, he uncovers a host of major cultural issues which have occupied criticism since his statement and indeed remain still unsolved.

In his studies of individual writers too, he offers some truly surprising contributions. He keeps alive a long-standing issue in the study of E. J. Pratt's poetry by positing a new and different reading by means of his analysis of stylistic issues in Pratt's work. He reads the tension in Atwood's work as one between a poetics of space and a poetics of time, tracing out the cultural implications of each and her paradoxical solution to contradictory impulses in her work. He distinguishes between the effects of the embodiment of magic and the disembodiment of magic (so to speak) in Gwendolyn MacEwen's poetry and fiction. He uncovers the Freudian implications of animal imagery in Sinclair Ross's fiction, a surprisingly rich reading of a writer not usually understood as involved in the tensions of sensuous experience.

In all this, Davey comes across as a writer devoted to a poetry and criticism alive at all points to the flux of experience and energetic awareness of motion and change. He opposes static form, the changeless structures of an art he would surely describe as lifeless, and praises everywhere the capacity that in the best art, as he would say, articulates the very pressure of time in its unceasing impulses through life. That concern with a phenomenological pressure makes itself evident particularly in two essays devoted to contemporary techniques and concerns: the image of the explorer in Western Canadian writing and the long poem essay. In both, Davey's alertness to the new directions of contemporary writing is evident as is his equally acute sense of historical pattern. His essay on the image of the explorer explores one of the major images of Western Canadian writing while his discussion of the long poem is a tour de force of critical insights and aperçu.

It has become clear recently that the long poem represents a major mode of contemporary writing. It had long seemed to our critics that there is something that could be spoken of as essentially Canadian in the genre of the long poem, though the terminology appropriate to it had not been settled upon. Northrop Frye's essay on "The Narrative Tradition in English-Canadian Poetry" foresaw as early as 1946 the importance of narrative form in the poetry of a new era in which technology would free the poem from the limited page, while in 1952 Frye connected the central problems of the poetry of the future with the technical problems of *Toward the Last Spike*. Dorothy Livesay wrote of *The Documentary: A Canadian Genre?* More recently, Robert Kroetsch set himself the task of discerning the distinguishing features of the long poem in a brilliant show of dialectal play. And in his anthology, *The Long Poem Anthology*, Michael Ondaatje provides not only examples of the long poem, but a skittish preface and invaluable comments by poets on their views of the form. Frank Davey's essay takes its place as another in these landmark statements about a form and direction for Canadian poetry.

Frank Davey's criticism...then,...represents an important addition to critical writing in Canada today....He belongs with those poet-critics who have given us their views of criticism and poetry, Miriam Waddington, George Bowering, Louis Dudek, D. G. Jones.

To critical theory he has added his voice on behalf of post-modern writing, and perhaps as clearly as any other writer has articulated the theory of post-modernism. He has given our criticism its contemporary voice, its sound and its rhythms, and to the mood of our most recent critical writing added his generous and welcoming spirit. A writer on the side of life, he has spoken for life and vitality as an active engaged spirit of our time.

Eli Mandel, York University

SURVIVING THE PARAPHRASE

It is a testimony to the limitations of Canadian literary criticism that thematic criticism should have become the dominant approach to English-Canadian literature. In its brief lifetime, Canadian criticism has acquired a history of being reluctant to focus on the literary work—to deal with matters of form, language, style, structure, and consciousness as these arise from the work as a unique construct. It has seldom had enough confidence in the work of Canadian writers to do what the criticism of other national literatures has done: explain and illuminate the work on its own terms, without recourse to any cultural rationalizations or apologies. Even the New Criticism's espousal of autotelic analysis did not move Canadian critics in this direction. Instead, in every period they have provided referential criticism: the evaluative criticism of Brown and Smith looks away from Canadian writing toward other national achievements; the anti-evaluative thematic criticism of Frye, Jones, Atwood, and Moss looks away toward alleged cultural influences and determiners.

With few critics interested in writing as writing, it is not surprising that Canada has in recent years seen the emergence of a large number of writer-critics. For unlike much earlier Canadian work, recent writing has been engaged for the most part at the level of form and language rather than theme. Rudy Wiebe's journey from *Peace Shall Destroy Many* to *The Temptations of Big Bear* has been an odyssey of novelistic technique about which thematic criticism can say very little. bp Nichol's *Two Novels* speaks only through its formal complexities, and until these are illuminated the thematic critic has to remain silent—as he has. At the moment it is Canadian writers who appear to have the greatest understanding of the technical concerns and accomplishments of their fellows, and it is these— Mandel, Waddington, Geddes, Barbour, Scobie, Bowering, Livesay—who are writing most of the periodical criticism that in any way comes to terms with the writing. Many of the academic critics (and I include here Douglas Jones and Margaret Atwood because of their acceptance of the thematic approach) appear almost as ignorant of movements in contemporary Canadian writing as their colleagues in the 1920s were of the formal experiments of Eliot, Pound, and Joyce.

Most of the weaknesses of thematic criticism stem from its origin in Arnoldian humanism, a tradition in which both the critic and the artist have a major responsibility to culture. In this view, the artist speaks, unconsciously or consciously, for the group. Says Jones, "[artists] participate in and help to articulate...a supreme fiction...that embodies the dreams and nightmares of a people, shapes their imaginative vision of the world, and defines, as it evolves, their cultural identity."[1] Language here is a tool employed not for its own intrinsic qualities but for the expression of ideas and visions. The critic's role is not to attend to language, form, or even to individual works of literature but to something called by Jones in *Butterfly on Rock* "our imaginative life," by Moss in his *Patterns of Isolation* the "national being,"[2] and by Frye in *The Bush Garden* "cultural history."[3]

At best these assumptions are extra-literary; at worst, anti-literary. The focus of such criticism invariably rests outside the writing—on "literature," "culture," geography, history and ideas. Books which begin ostensibly as attempts to illuminate separate instances of Canadian writing become messianic attempts to define a national identity or psychosis. The critical process produced by these assumptions is reductive. A novel is reduced to its declared themes and its plot outline; a poem to its declared themes; the Canadian culture ultimately to catch-words such as Atwood's "victimization" and "survival." Critical analysis is performed mostly to derive new catch-words and formulae.

The movement here is towards paraphrase—paraphrase of the culture and paraphrase of the literature. The critic extracts for his deliberations the paraphrasable content and throws away the form. He attends to the explicit meaning of the work and neglects whatever content is implicit in its structure, language or imagery. Thus Atwood discusses the overt attacks on puritanism in Marian Engel's *The Honeymoon Festival*, but makes no comment about the novel's two most arresting technical features: its low-key style (common to all of Engel's fiction) and its unlikely, perhaps incredible, conclusion. Douglas Jones quotes lengthy passages from F.R. Scott and Patrick Anderson in order to integrate into his thesis their explicit statements on Canadian culture, but has no comment about their direct and largely denotative use of language. My objection here is based on a principle formulated by Frye: "the literary structure is always ironic because 'what it says' is always different from 'what it means.'"[4] Thematic critics in Canada have been interested in what literary works "say," especially what they "say" about Canada and Canadians. They have largely overlooked what literary works "mean"—for the attempt to establish meaning would take them outside thematic criticism. As Robert Creeley has remarked,

> ...it cannot be simply what a man proposes to talk about in a poem that is interesting—this is like going to hear an after-dinner speaker. His information will be interesting just to the extent that it exists, but after that we are through with him and through with the information in the form that he has given it to

> us. But the poem has this informational character...in such form that we don't throw away the poem. In other words, after we've read a play by Shakespeare, let's say, we don't throw away the play. We continue to define what is said/happening in how it is said.[5]

Since Frye's genuinely thematic criticism of Canadian literature constitutes a small body of work (less than half of *The Bush Garden*), since Moss' criticism is largely derivative of Frye and Jones, and since my opinion of Atwood's *Survival* is on record elsewhere,[6] I will restrict my detailed comments about thematic criticism here to Douglas Jones' *Butterfly on Rock*. One of the first characteristics of thematic criticism that one notices in this book is the humanistic bias. To Jones, culture is a gentleman's club inside which any member can speak piously on behalf of the rest of the group.

> ...our westward expansion is complete, and in the pause to reflect upon ourselves we become increasingly aware that our identity and our view of the world are no longer determined by our experience of Europe.[7]

Apparently no one is allowed by Jones to detach himself from this rather arrogant humanistic assumption of corporateness of society. The assumption leads to further difficulties when extended to writing; the literary work comes to have little significance outside the body of the national literature. It can be valued not for its unique or idiosyncratic qualities but only for what it shares with the larger body. This means, in effect, that the derivative and the mundane can receive the critic's attention while the unusual or original do not. The eccentric Robertson Davies, for instance, does not get a mention in Jones. Such a situation parallels the effect of humanism on society and culture where whatever coincides with mass-values is tolerated and whatever conflicts is rejected or ignored.

A second feature of thematic criticism evident in Jones is a disregard for literary history. Atwood develops her thesis that victimization is a characteristic theme of Canadian literature by ignoring its ubiquity in contemporary world literature. Moss develops his thesis that isolation is the major theme of Canadian fiction by overlooking, as George Woodcock has noted,[8] the fact that in all literatures the traditional subject of the novel has been the person who is "isolated" by his not being able to fit comfortably into society. Similarly, Jones tries to advance, on the basis of work by the Confederation Poets, the thesis that the Canadian landscape has been seen as "a savage place...holy and enchanted"—ignoring the documented fact that the ghostly presences in Carman, Lampman, and Roberts were inherited from English Romanticism and American Transcendentalism rather than gained osmotically from the Canadian condition. In each case the critic is forced into ignoring literary history by a paradox unique to his critical approach. Thematic criticism in Canada seeks above all to define a national culture but chooses to work with materials—literary themes—that are, because of their limited number, international in nature. The paradox creates a dilemma from which there appears to be no scholarly escape.

A third feature is thematic criticism's tendency toward sociology—usually bad sociology. While the social scientist is content to describe society and predict the effects of specific events or interventions, Jones attempts both to describe Canadian culture and to prescribe how it should change. His sociology is extra-literary, normative and polemic. His declared aim is to locate a culture "in which the Canadian will feel at home in his world" and abandon his "colonial mentality."

> The weakness of the colonial mentality is that it regards as a threat what it should regard as its salvation; it walls out or exploits what it should welcome and cultivate.[9]

This unscholarly approach leads Jones eventually to cast himself as a Canadian Adam who can announce to Canadians the end of exile and the discovery of "the first days of Creation."

A fourth feature is an attempt at "culture-fixing"— something very common of late in Canada in such books as Purdy's *The New*

Romans, Kilbourn's *The Peaceable Kingdom*, Redekop's *The Star-Spangled Beaver*, Frye's *The Bush Garden*, Fulford, Godfrey and Rotstein's *Read Canadian*, and Atwood's *Survival*. To Jones, Canadian culture is in transition from an Old Testament condition of exile and alienation toward a New Testament one of affirmation, discovery, and community. This metaphor for the Canadian experience dominates *Butterfly on Rock* and becomes, much like Atwood's victim/victimization concept, a formula for Canadianism. Like all formulae, it is a restricting and potentially paralyzing thing. It restricts the writers who Jones can discuss; they are necessarily selected by their suitability to the thesis rather than by the quality of their writing. It is potentially paralyzing in the way that any attempt to define the Canadian subject must be—it serves to intimidate future Canadian writing into taking as its own the particular concerns that have been declared officially Canadian.

A fifth feature which Jones has in common with other thematic critics is the fallacy of literary determinism. The artist "embodies the dreams and nightmares of a people"; his work can be "explained" by reference to the geography and climate of the country, to western intellectual history, to his culture's religious heritage. Jones is much less guilty of this fallacy than is Frye in *The Bush Garden* with his reference to the "bleak northern sky" and to the St. Lawrence River's swallowing of travellers into "an alien continent," but he nevertheless fails to make clear that the writer is in some small way free, that the writer chooses among influences and traditions rather than being passively formed by them, and that this process of election is more important to an understanding of literature than the influence or tradition itself. As Gaston Bachelard has observed, to "explain" a work by its sources is tantamount to explaining "the flower by the fertilizer."[10] But of course thematic criticism is not principally interested in the artistic process, in the artist, or in the literary work—its interest lies, as Jones states, in things "cultural and psychological rather than purely aesthetic or literary."

The motivations of thematic criticism strike one as essentially defensive in respect to both the culture and the literature. A declared motive has been to avoid evaluative criticism, which Frye had claimed would reduce Canadian criticism to a "huge debunking project." An even more important but undeclared motive appears to have been to avoid treating Canadian writing as serious literature. For there are many kinds of non-evaluative criticism which these critics could have practised other than the thematic. It seems that the thematicists believe Canadian literature incapable of sustaining analytic, phenomenological, or archetypal inquiry—of sustaining any kind of criticism whose existence is not also supported by the ruse of sociological research. Another declared motive has been to articulate a cultural identity to a nation which the thematic critic believes convinced of its lack of one. It is noteworthy here that the thematicists' concerns—Jones' quest for "the obscure features of our own identity," Moss' for "a coherent body of Canadian fiction," Atwood's for "a single unifying and informing [Canadian] symbol"[11]—are not those of critics of more mature and secure literatures. One cannot imagine a British critic being worried about what constitutes, in a word or less, the essence of his literature. Instead, he goes about its illumination, writing books with such titles as *New Bearings in English Poetry*, *A Key to Modern English Poetry*, *Four Metaphysical Poets*, *The English Novel*. Much more effective than *Butterfly on Rock*, *The Bush Garden*, *Survival*, and *Patterns of Isolation* in asserting a Canadian identity would have been books of this British type— books which assumed, rather than argued, a national identity's existence and a national literature's significance.

It is essential that Canadian critics not forget that there are alternatives to thematic criticism, and that most of these do not involve a return to that *bête noire* evaluation. Further, these alternatives, like thematic criticism, do allow the writing of overviews of all or parts of Canadian literature. But unlike thematic criticism, they attend specifically to that ground from which all writing communicates and all themes spring: the form—style, structure, vocabulary, literary form, syntax—of the writing. One such alternative, historical criticism, could provide a history of Canadian poetry—a history not of its themes and concerns but of its technical assumptions, the sources of these assumptions, and the relationship prosody of Canadian writers and that of other Western writers. While the prosody of Canadian poets undoubtedly has been mostly derivative, there have been shifts in the ingenuousness of the borrowing, in the time-lapse between the model and its imitation, in the sources of the models, and in the amount and significance of the modifications contributed by the borrower. All writing is to some extent derivative, but there would appear to be a clear division in Canadian poetry between obsequious borrowing—for example, that of Mair of Roberts—and the intelligent combining and expansion of borrowed forms. Needless to say, one by-product of such a non-thematic study would be an implicit statement about Canadians, Canada, and its evolution.

Analytical criticism could yield such works as "Modernism in Canadian Poetry" or "Discontinuous Structure in Post-Modern Canadian Writing." The former would not only address itself to the late appearance of the modernist movement in Canada—some thirty years after its appearance in Hispano-American literature and fifteen years after its appearance in Anglo-American literature—but inquire into the formal characteristics which distinguish Canadian modernism from its sister movements. Hispano-American modernism was anti-colonial in spirit; its rejection of European models in favour of native forms led artists eventually to primitivism; Anglo-American modernism was anti-Georgian and, from an American point of view, also anti-colonial. Canadian modernism, in the work of Smith, Scott, Gustafson, and Finch, copied the Anglo-Americans in both theory and practice; it proposed, unlike the South Americans, "cosmopolitan" models rather than regional ones, and to this extent seems to have been a colonial movement. My point here is that a colonial, imitative modernist movement is not to be deplored or rationalized into something other. It is itself an intrinsically interesting literary phenomenon, and in an absolute sense worthy of analysis and study; such a study can be done in terms of Canadian literature as successfully as it can in terms of any other.[12]

The second analytical project, "Discontinuous Structure in Post-Modern Canadian Writing," could directly attempt, on the basis of Canadian literature, an elucidation of the problems and advantages of discontinuous literary structure. Such structure has been at the core of most significant new writing in Canada in the last decade: Rudy Wiebe's *The Blue Mountains of China*, David McFadden's *The Great Canadian Sonnet*, Leonard Cohen's *Beautiful Losers*, Gerry Gilbert's *AND*, bp Nichol's *The Martyrology*, Juan Butler's *The Garbageman*, to name a few. While it would be absurd to argue that Canada has had any kind of monopoly or "lead" in such writing, the opportunity nevertheless exists for a literary problem important to all literatures to be usefully discussed strictly in terms of Canadian writing. The literature would provide the critic with a rich stock of relevant writing and a compact, clearly defined area for investigation.

Were genre criticism to attempt a work such as "The Polemic Novel in Canadian Literature," the same procedure would be involved; that is, of discussing on the basis of Canadian writing a literary issue of para-national interest. Here I am not asking for a repetition of thematic criticism's numerous discussions of the ideas of these novels, but for an examination of them as examples of a literary form—for an examination of their language, usual methods of characterization, narrative techniques, etc. The polemic novel exists throughout Canadian literature in abundance, with Kirby's *Chien d'Or*, several of Connor's works, Duncan's *The Imperialist*, Callaghan's *Such Is My Beloved*, McLennan's *Two Solitudes*, Wiebe's *Peace Shall Destroy Many*, Atwood's *Surfacing*, Clark's *Storm of Fortune*, and Richler's *The Incomparable Atuk* being among the stronger. Having had such an unusually large hold on Canadian fiction, it could, like derivative modernism or discontinuous form, be studied as thoroughly through Canadian literature as through any other body of national work. Such a claim does not imply that these Canadian novels are "great" novels; only that they form a more adequate basis for serious literary study and deserve to be so treated.

Phenomenological criticism is another alternative, non-evaluative approach which could do much to replace the present sociological perspective that dominates Canadian criticism with a literary one. Again, the essential assumption would be that Canadian literature is a highly useful frame of reference for approaching particular literary problems. One title which the phenomenologist could produce— and here again no derogation would be intended by the word "colonial"—is "The Colonial Writing Experience." From Mair and Heavysege to Smith and Richler, our writers have given literary form to the experience of living and writing in terms of values imposed by non-native cultures. The phenomenological critic could study how this experience is projected by the form of the writing, could participate in the consciousness of the artist as it is betrayed by his syntax, imagery, and diction; ultimately the critic could give the reader a portrait of each writer's psychological world. Another possible project for this kind of criticism is "The Regional Consciousness in Canadian Writing." In regional literature too, Canada has a more than sufficient body of work for the study of a particular, intrinsically interesting literary phenomenon. In fact, it is not unfair to say that the bulk of Canadian literature is regional before it is national— despite whatever claims Ontario or Toronto writers may make to represent a national vision. The regional consciousness may be characterized by specific attitudes to language and form, by specific kinds of imagery, or by language and imagery that in some ways correlate with the geographic features of the region. The analyses in Atwood's *Survival*, for example, despite the book's ignoring of regional factors, imply a possible prepossession with closed space in Southern Ontario writing and with the closing of space in Prairie writing. These leads call for further investigation.

A final type of criticism which might be practised profitably by Canadian critics is archetypal criticism which, despite the eminence of Northrop Frye, has never been applied in its pure form to Canadian writing. Frye's "theory of modes" would supply an especially interesting approach to a literature which has seen in recent years a curiously large number of attempts at high-mimetic art—including Newlove's "The Pride," Gutteride's *Riel*, Cohen's *Beautiful Losers*, Nichol's *The Marty-*

rology, MacEwen's *King of Egypt, King of Dreams* and Wiebe's *The Temptations of Big Bear*. Possibly Frye's theory of an evolution from high mimesis to mimesis to irony does not fit Canadian literature; perhaps in literatures which lack a native high-mimetic inheritance writers are stimulated to attempt such writing despite living in ages in which international writing is overwhelmingly mimetic or ironic. Only an archetypal examination of the language and structures used in Canadian and other recently-developed literatures could confirm such hypotheses.

Unless these or similar critical alternatives are taken up, there is a danger that the shape of the literature could suffer long-term distortion. Thematic criticism does not use, or need to use, literary criteria in selecting writers to document its arguments. It selects writers not in terms of literary competence or talent but in terms of how well their work fits the critic's particular thematic thesis. While one may agree with Frye that evaluation is the "incidental by-product" of criticism rather than its end, one finds that the by-product of thematic criticism is the creation of the illusion that palpably inferior writers are somehow more important—at least to loyal Canadians—than obviously superior ones. Thus Atwood makes Dennis Lee appear more significant than Irving Layton, and Graeme Gibson more significant than Margaret Laurence; Jones makes Patrick Anderson and Phyllis Webb appear more significant than Dorothy Livesay; Moss makes Charles Bruce and Thomas H. Raddall appear more accomplished than Robert Kroetsch, Hugh Hood, or Robertson Davies. The only criticism which can yield the kind of critical by-products which Frye has in mind is one which focusses not on sociological issues but on the writing itself. Here no writer can be excluded because of his attitudes or subject matter. All competent uses of literary form can enter into the deliberations of the historical, analytic, genre, phenomenological, or archetypal critic. The more profound uses rise to prominence because of their power, complexity, and ingenuity. Thematic criticism searches for apples among oranges by looking for cultural seers among men and women whose principal task is articulation and whose principal loyalty is to their language; these alternative kinds of criticism would turn the critic's attention back to where the writer's must always be—on literature as language, and on writing as writing.

---

1. *Butterfly on Rock* (Toronto: University of Toronto Press, 1970), p. 4.

2. (Toronto: McClelland & Stewart, 1974), p. 7.

3. (Toronto: House of Anansi, 1971), p. 215.

4. *Anatomy of Criticism* (Princeton University Press, 1957), p. 81.

5. Tape-recorded lecture at home of Warren Tallman, Vancouver, B.C., August 29, 1962.

6. "Atwood Walking Wackwards," *Open Letter* (second series) 5 (Summer 1973), 74-84.

7. *Butterfly on Rock*, p. 3.

8. "Isolating a Theme in our Fiction," *Maclean's*, April 1974, p. 96.

9. *Butterfly on Rock*, p. 7.

10. *The Poetics of Space*, tr. Maria Jolas (Boston: Beacon Press, 1969), p. xxvi.

11. *Survival* (Toronto: House of Anansi, 1972), p. 31.

12. For another example of the analytical approach to colonial writing see William D. Gairdner's article, "Traill and Moodie: The Two Realities," *The Journal of Canadian Fiction*, 1:2 (Spring, 1972).

E. J. PRATT: APOSTLE OF CORPORATE MAN

The vision of E. J. Pratt has provided the major area for dispute among critics. Early commentators such as John Sutherland,[1] Desmond Pacey,[2] and Northrop Frye,[3] saw Pratt as a Christian humanist; to Vincent Sharman in 1964 he seems to have been an atheist;[4] and to Peter Buitenhuis, editor of the recent *Selected Poems*, both of these views represent misreadings of Pratt's work. In Buitenhuis' opinion Pratt is a man drawn "toward relativism and agnosticism."[5] In the general stressing of Pratt's religious views, the importance of Frye's observation that Pratt is a "spokesman rather than a critic of public opinion and generally accepted social reactions"[6] has been largely overlooked. It was reiterated by Fred Cogswell in 1964, but not as pointing the direction to the key aspects of Pratt's world-view. "The conception of heroism in Pratt is of the kind that belongs to our age, to an industrial democracy," said Frye. Continued Cogswell, "he [Pratt] is the poet... of mass action over individual action."[8]

Stated briefly, the problems which have so far engaged Pratt critics are two: the first, what is his poetry about, and the second, what world-view does this poetry project? The convolutions of some of the early critics, notably John Sutherland, to get the 'right' answer to the first question have been adequately exposed and documented by Earle Birney.[9] But even Peter Buitenhuis shies from the obvious answers that Pratt's subject matter may be no more than the stories he tells and that his vision may be no more than the values which his protagonists embody. A careful reading of Pratt's work, in fact, suggests very strongly that Pratt was much more straightforward as an artist than most of his sophisticated critics care to admit. He seems to have been seldom concerned with such profound questions as are easily raised by too analytical an approach to his work. Is a whale ("The Cachalot") more to be admired than Pratt's brave fellow Newfoundlanders who die pursuing it? Is "the great Panjandrum" ("The Truant") also the god that awaits Pratt's mother behind *The Iron Door?* Can the ship *Titanic* be an instance of *hubris* when the locomotive, "The 6000," is not? Are the priest of the *Roosevelt* and the saintly Brébeuf both 'truants'? Can the K-148 ("The Submarine") be eulogized for its 'mechanic power' while German armoured vehicles are declared "crueller than the hordes of Tamburlaine"?[10]

Although these and other ambiguities in Pratt's work can be resolved if considered as peripheral to one simple and pervasive idea in Pratt, his critics have been thrown by them into confusion. Not only are such ambiguities responsible for the Christian humanist-atheist-agnostic controversy, but for his "Tyrannosaurus Rex" ("The Great Feud") being Christ to Sutherland and "mere instinctive physical courage" to Desmond Pacey, for his cachalot being "heroic energy"[11] to Pacey but thoroughly a whale to Earle Birney,[12] and for *The Iron Door* being pessimistic to Vincent Sharman[13] but optimistic to Peter Buitenhuis.[14] And while Frye can call Pratt a defender of "generally accepted social reactions,"[15] Pacey can state, "Pratt obviously believes that all worthwhile human achievement rests not on conformity but on non-conformity."[16] No wonder Pacey is led to declare, "I suspect that a good deal of the ambiguity in Pratt is not deliberate but involuntary, and that there is not only confusion among critics but also confusion in the poet."[17]

Once one gets past the confusions of the critics, from John Sutherland's fantastic system-building to Vincent Sharman's humorously perverse interpretation of *Brébeuf and his Brethren,*[18] and begins a direct reading of the text of Pratt's poems, one sees Pacey as having been most correct in terming them "deceptively simple."[19] But, unfortunately for Mr. Pacey and his brethren, this simplicity is deceptive not in masking something more complex but merely in being, disappointingly, no more than itself. Pratt's shark ("The Shark") is only a shark, admirable for its latent and impersonal power. Pratt's cachalot is an aggressive and virile whale, stunning in its inherited energy and strength, but referential to no symbolic meaning outside itself. His Brébeuf is not remarkable either as a Christian or as a Christ-figure, but as an instance of the power to be gained by an individual through allegiance to the ideals of a group. The Jesuits are more impressive to Pratt as power-figures than are the Indians because the odds are higher against them and thus more demanding of power. Similarly, in *Dunkirk* the strength of the British infantry is more admirable than that of the German Panzers, and in *Behind the Log* the strength of the beleaguered convoy is more admirable than that of the relatively secure U-boats.

Power is one of the keys to Pratt's uncomplicated vision. He is fascinated by power much the way contemporary man has been fascinated by powerful automobiles and tempted to identify vicariously with them. Further, Pratt displays our culture's love of the underdog, believing along with this culture that the underdog somehow marshals more impressive power in either victory or defeat than any favourite can. Thus Pratt's sympathy for the dying cachalot, for the tortured Brébeuf and Lalement, for the battered sailors of the *Roosevelt* and the *Antinoe,* for the *Orillia* in *Behind the Log,* for the harassed John A. Macdonald in *Towards the Last Spike,* for "the truant," or again for the British rear-guard at Dunkirk. And thus also Pratt's scorn for the crew and passengers of the *Titanic,* who would, had they managed themselves properly, have had all in their favour, and conversely his reverent awe for that "grey shape with the palaeolithic face."

Pratt's vision, unlike Brébeuf's, is unashamedly worldly. The power he respects and eulogizes is nearly always power wielded or shared in the here and now by inhabitants of this world. Divine power is contrastingly unimpressive to Pratt. He has only the vaguest sense of what stretches beyond 'the iron door'; he sees the power of the *Roosevelt's* priest as over-shadowed by that of her sailors, the power of "the great Panjandrum" as totally overshadowed by that of the audacious and worldly "truant." Only in the very moving opening pages of *Brébeuf and his Brethren* does the Protestant Pratt exhibit any sensitivity in the mysteries of the divine, and here only because his common-sense attitudes have been forced to yield to the artistic necessity of identifying with the Catholic hero.

Werner Sombart[20] and R. H. Tawney[21] have convincingly documented how modern capitalism had its birth in medieval scholasticism and Protestant secularization of the scholastic method. Tawney in particular has demonstrated how Protestantism in Western culture has been the prerequisite for a common-sense handling of reality, a respect for worldly power, and a high valuation of the ability to manipulate material objects. It is this complex of characteristics that we see in the attitudes of E. J. Pratt: a respect for raw material power ("The Shark," "The Submarine," "The 6000"), a complete and disciplined attention to things of this world (*Behind the Log, Towards the Last Spike*), and, except briefly in *Brébeuf*, a blind eye for mystery and eternity. From the Renaissance through the eighteenth century such a world-view energized the mercantilist sensibility so well recorded by Defoe. In the nineteenth century it allied itself with Spencer's distortions of Darwinian theory and secured prolonged life for *laissez-faire* economics. In the twentieth century it seeks yet more worldly power for the 'truant' human race through the mechanical excesses of corporate exterprise. As Marshall McLuhan reported in *The Mechanical Bride:*

> The puritan both retained the scholastic method in theology and gave it expression in the precision and austerity of his secular existence. So that it is scarcely fantastic to say that a great modern

> business is a secular adaptation of the most striking features of medieval scholastic culture. Confronted with the clockwork precision of scholastic method, Lewis Mumford could think only of the mechanical parallel of a smoothly working textile plant. The object of this systematic process is now production and finance rather than God.[22]

And with corporate enterprise we have entered deeply into the world of E. J. Pratt. What are the gods of this world but organization, planning, efficiency, regimentation, discipline, and order? To Pratt, nature has this order and efficiency. This is implicit in the fish analogy of "The Submarine," in his account of the architecture of the cachalot, in the 'metallic teeth' of "The Shark," in the very waves which "crashed down in volleys flush against the hull" of the *Roosevelt*; it is, in fact, inscribed deep within the iceberg's 'palaeolithic face.' Men, in Pratt's view, acquire such order and efficiency not as individuals but as members of corporate groups. This, as we shall see, is the message of *The Titanic, Brébeuf and his Brethren, Towards the Last Spike,* and many other of the poet's works.

Pratt seems to have the distinction among modern poets of being an enemy of individual action. One of the few characters in Pratt who acts not as an agent of society or member of a social order is the seaman Uno Wertanen of the *Roosevelt.* This momentary action, however, is both unwitting and unwanted.

> The crew could see him grab and plunge and cling,
> Using his legs as a rudder so to swing
> Her head around to the wreck and with sheer
> Abandon of his youth to try to steer
> His open, wilful, single-handed craft...

Markedly isolated, even exiled, by storm and accident from his social group, Wertanen drowns. Other individualists in Pratt are the seal-hunters of *The Eagle* who are cut off from their social order by a blizzard which catches them out upon the ice. Here, deprived of the structure and power of society, the individual human being is capable of surviving.

> ...like sheep we huddled and broke
> Here one would fall as hunger took hold
> Of his step; here one would sleep as the cold
> Crept into his blood, and another would kneel
> Athwart the body of some dead seal,
> And with knife and nails would tear it apart
> To flesh his teeth in its frozen heart,
> And another dreamed that the storm was past
> And raved of his bunk and brandy and food....
>
> ("The Ice Floes")

The most blatant individualist in all of Pratt's work is "The Brawler in Who's Who." Acknowledged for individual heroism by "two DSO's," the brawler has come to this achievement through murdering his infant brother and his mother, through making "a Bedlam" of his schools, and through fighting in war like the Tyrannosaurus Rex of "The Great Feud." In this poem Pratt clearly links individual heroism both with seriously antisocial behaviour and with diminished chances for survival. The brawler, who has dissociated himself from the protection of the social order, dies in the middle of life, murdered.

In contrast to the people above, individual men in Pratt who act as loyal members of a group acquire the possibility not only of survival but also of participating in great and laudable deeds. To the modern reader, schooled to resent oppression of the individual by 'bureaucracies' or 'establishments' of any sort, Pratt's quotation from the seamen's contract at the opening of *The Roosevelt and the Antinoe* is mildly humorous.

> ...they, the crew
> Should pledge themselves to conduct, *faithful, true,*
> *And orderly, in honest, sober manner;*
> *At all times in their duties diligent;*

To the master's lawful word obedient,
In everything relating to the vessel—
Safety of passengers, cargo, and store,
Whether on board, in boats, or on the shore.

Yet to Pratt this passage underlines a frame of mind essential to the heroism which is later to be displayed by the crew. In this poem even the radio stations have an almost sentimentalized social responsibility.

Thousands of dials in studio and station
Were 'off the air' by an ungrudged consent—
That the six-hundred-metre wave might keep
Upon the sea that night its high command.

Throughout Pratt's work there is a pervasive theme of collective action, of strength gained by identification with a group or cause. In "The Great Feud" disaster befalls the land dwellers when they ignore the ape's command,

But as their allies, ye shall spend,
In one grand consummating blow
Of death against the common foe,
Your strength to a triumphant end,

and fall into lethal internecine struggle. This calamity is precipitated by another of Pratt's unfortunate individualists, Tyrannosaurus Rex, whose folly is that he will affiliate with neither side but instead battles both groups on his own. In "The Cachalot" all of the individuals involved in the final struggle can identify with an order larger than themselves. The whalers form a traditional sea-going social unit, and the cachalot, Pratt is eager to tell us, can trace back his ancestry "a thousand years." The whale's particular greatness is informed by ancestors that had followed Lief Ericsson, Marco Polo, Columbus, da Gama, "Cortez, Cavendish, and Drake," that had sunk a Dutch battleship in the English Channel and a British one at Trafalgar. *Dunkirk* is similarly a poem not about individuals, but also about a social group, a nation, extending both in numbers like the whaler's crew and in history like the cachalot's ancestors.

> Milleniums it had taken to make their stock.
> Piltdown hung on the frontals of their fathers.
> They had lain as sacrifices
> Upon the mortuary slabs of Stonehenge...
> They had signed up with Frobisher,
> Had stifled cries in the cockpits of Trafalgar.
> They had emptied their veins into the Marne.

In *Behind the Log* and *Towards the Last Spike*, Pratt's emphasis on the collective nature of the great successes of man is already well known, being noted by both Frye[23] and Buitenhuis.[24] From the Commodore's warning that in the convoy "there is but little room/For rugged individualists" to the poet's observation that the battle was fought by "men with surnames blotted by their jobs/into a scrawl of anonymity," *Behind the Log* is a story of ships rather than of men, of corporate heroism rather than of individual bravery. The Commodore himself does little more than co-operate in the general flow of events. In *Towards the Last Spike* Pratt celebrates another instance of collective action. Here, in a superficial reading, either Macdonald or Van Horne can appear as a hero. Yet once again Pratt makes the network of interaction and interdependency abundantly clear. Van Horne supports Macdonald, and Macdonald reciprocates. Both men are further supported by Tupper, Stephen, and Smith, and all five are in turn reliant on the loyalty, sweat, and ingenuity of the thousands of workers who, in dedication to their task, "...lost their identity; as groups/As gangs, they massed, divided, subdivided/Like numerals only...."

Even *Brébeuf and his Brethren* loses much of the complexity which has puzzled critics from John Sutherland to Vincent Sharman when it is regarded as merely another Prattian eulogy of the power gained by men when they unite hierarchically in a common belief to a common purpose. The Christianity and the Catholicism of Brébeuf and the other priests are essentially peripheral to the central meaning of the poem. These are merely parts of the vision which binds the participants to their tasks, and, as such, are parallel to the goal of the sea-to-sea railway in *Towards the Last Spike* or the goal of convoy survival in *Behind the Log*. Thus both Sharman's questioning of Pratt's attitude to Christianity in the poem and Sutherland's desire to show the poem as optimistically Christian are relatively unimportant. What is important in considering *Brébeuf and his Brethren* is the fact that Pratt admires any kind of heroic collective action against long odds, whether it be against the sea, the Nazis, the mountains, or the heathen—or even, as in "The Truant," against "the great Panjundrum himself."

Throughout *Brébeuf and his Brethren* what seems most striking to Pratt is that Brébeuf does not act as an individual. He is before all else a member of a corporate body, the Jesuit order, and as such is informed by "the winds of God" which are blowing into the hearts of many men at this time across Europe. Further, he is directly informed by divine presence, a "Real Presence"—by his vision of "a bleeding form/Falling beneath the instrument of death." Thus he is more than the agent of a holy order; he is the agent of divine will as well. Knowing that he may face martyrdom in the New World, Brébeuf studies the temptations that such a fate can offer. What is the chief temptation?-that of "the brawler," individual glory. Here Brébeuf learns the lesson of Eliot's Becket, that martyrdom must not be sought for its own sake but only encountered through performing "the will of God."

The theme of "French imperialism in North America" noted by Buitenhuis[25] seems to be present in the poem only to heighten the impression that Brébeuf is no more than a participant in a complex of events much larger than himself. Note how his name here is only one on a list of makers in a great enterprise.

New France restored! Champlain, Masse, Brébeuf
Were in Quebec, hopes riding high as ever.

> Davost and Daniel soon arrived to join
> The expedition west. Midsummer tide,
> The busiest the Colony had ever known,
> Was over: forty-three canoes to meet
> The hazards of return;...

And as Brébeuf is carried by these events, he is admired by Pratt largely because he is worthy of them, because he is loyal to the vast movements which are giving his life its significance. As the Commodore and the sailors serve the convoy, and as Macdonald and the navvies serve the building of the CPR, Brébeuf serves the tide of French Christianity to which he has pledged himself. He suffers in smoky hovels, he tricks the Indians with predictions of eclipses and rainfall, he faces death at the hands of the Neutrals, eats the filthy food of the Hurons, all for the enlargement of the Catholic community. Says Pratt, "But never could the Indians infer/Self-gain or anything but simple courage/Inspired by a zeal beyond reproof,..."

This is the loyalty which Pratt admires in men, the loyalty of 'simple' courage, the submission of individual will to group projects significantly greater than oneself. The glory that Pratt admires is not that of the defiant individual but that of the defiant group (his "truant," after all, is generic), which can be vicariously enjoyed by the individual either in a sacrificial death or a participatory triumph. The cachalot fights and dies for the glory of his race; Brébeuf fights and dies for the glory of his faith; the weekend sailors at Dunkirk fight and win for the glory of England. Today this kind of glory is the kind offered by large corporations to their loyal employees. Again Marshall McLuhan can describe the process:

> Great physical and industrial power rests on a multitude of powerless individuals, many of whom are deeply resentful of their condition. The smaller and meaner the man, the more he craves to possess not limited human powers, with all the effort of cultivation and all the responsibility that implies, but superhuman power. (That is the meaning of the Squinky comic

> books, and of "Superman.") The sadistic craving for enormous physical powers to revenge or compensate for human futility will always drive such people to link themselves to vast impersonal enterprises. They will follow automatically any road which promises to bring them to that goal. So that to be a switch thrower in a *big* plant looks better to them than any lonely task, however human. Such is also the attraction of bureaucratic jobs, whether in great corporations or in government. It is by fantasy identification with the very big power unit that the very small man obtains his self-realization as a superman. The key to Superman is Clark Kent the useless. Therefore the more we create the means to centralize physical power, the more we suppress our human nature; and then that human nature queues up all the more to support the big physical power that crushes it.

This is the fate of Brébeuf, of the nameless sailors of Convoy SC42, of the masses who built the CPR, even of the cachalot: to achieve greatness only as agents of oppressively vast powers, forces, traditions. It is a fate based on a principle very similar to that 'old lie' of Wilfrid Owen's "Dulce et Decorum Est." It is a fate which McLuhan terms "a nightmare dream"[26] but which Pratt consistently recommends.

Pratt's story of the *Titanic* is the story of the consequences of man's failure to live up to tradition and duty, of his failure to exhibit Conradian restraint and solidarity upon the sea. In Pratt, machinery requires for its management the utmost in disciplined civilized values. Men welded together as a unit operate the successful K-148 ("The Submarine"), row the *Roosevelt's* lifeboats to the *Antinoe*, lay the rails of the CPR, and save Convoy SC42. On the *Titanic* men have become so dazzled by the qualities of the machine with which they have been entrusted that they fail to be worthy of this trust. They over-estimate this machine's capabilities much as Ulysses' men over-estimated human capabilities when they "would have slain the cattle of the sun." Thus the *Titanic's* crew believe that "caution was absurd" and disregard the disciplined management necessary for any ship's safety.

Throughout the poem the *Titanic's* crew's aloofness and difference from the crews of other ships are clearly developed. While the *Caronia, Mesaba, Amerika, Baltic, Touraine,* and *Californian* pick their ways gingerly through the "ice-field," the *Titanic* increases speed as it approaches. And while these ships, particularly the *Californian,* fulfil their social duties by warning all other ships at sea, the *Titanic* declares itself superciliously above this moral solidarity of all good sailors. "Say, 'California,' shut up, keep out/You're jamming all my signals with Cape Race."

The *Titanic's* passengers share in this divorce between human responsibility and the demands of machine and sea. The tread of the passengers' feet, we are told, is "rivalling the engines." The diners approach the ship's diningroom "like storm troops before a citadel." So remote are the passengers from the requirements of discipline, attention, and duty at sea that some of them suggest the crew to be superfluous. "For all the hard work there's to do/Aboard this liner up on deck, the crew/ Might just as well have stopped ashore." Even less concern for solidarity and for human action in a corporate body is shown by the passengers in their relationships with their fellow men. Physical violence is latent in the wrestling and boxing displays in the ship's gymnasium. Animosity and rapaciousness only just below the level of physical violence are continually evident in Cabin D's poker game. Meanwhile the "grey-templed Caesars of the world's Exchange" have gathered in the lounge to use their collective wisdom not for social good but to "rock/the pillared dollars of a railroad stock." Representative of this general nonobservance of obligation to the social order is the Egyptian mummy in the hold. Stolen from a tomb in the Valley of the Kings in direct contravention of not only a respect for the human dead but also of the mores of another civilization, this mummy is rumoured to carry with it "an ancient curse" on all violaters of the necessary mores which bind men together and make possible their survival on earth. It is noteworthy that Pratt does not question the credulity of the passengers who discuss this mummy and its "curse," but presents their dialogue with the same profound fascination as he presents the other events of the poem.

Once the iceberg has punctured the illusion of the crew and passengers that social irresponsibility is a condition possible for man, there is a marked return among these people to the old loyalties. Captain Smith regains a captain's wisdom in his managing of the ship's abandonment so that panic and violence do not interfere with the orderly evacuation of women and children. In playing until the sea silences their instruments, the seven musicians exhibit a fidelity which, in the ship's officers, could earlier have saved the ship. Among the passengers also a selfless heroism takes hold, not only among those anonymous masses "of unknown name/and race" who impressed Pratt in *Behind the Log* and *Towards the Last Spike*, but also among those rulers of the stock exchange, Guggenheim and Astor. Thus the story of the *Titanic* is, like Pratt's other major narrative poems, a story of the necessity of social responsibility, of group action and group heroism, of men uniting in a common cause and gaining strength and inspiration from their own communality.

This theme of *The Titanic* is clearly the single most powerful constant of Pratt's poetry. It surpasses in importance both his theme of power and his intermittent theme of Christian love in that it subsumes both of these. It is through corporate action that power, both effective power and individual power, is realized. Christianity itself, especially in *Brébeuf and his Brethren*, is merely one more means of binding men together and giving to the individual totemistic or institutional support.

The question of whether this philosophy of Pratt's was felt by him to be relevant only to crisis situations or to all of human life has been raised by Northrop Frye, who, in suggesting the former, observed that Pratt "is almost always dealing with a society in a state of emergency."[27] This observation seems both insufficient for the conclusion and an over-statement of the case. The everyday building of the CPR did not constitute a 'crisis' to the ordinary labourer, and yet Pratt definitely expects a continuing loyalty and efficiency from him. In the case of the *Titanic* the time period in which communality is lacking is that immediately preceding the crisis. Here Pratt's implication would seem to be that society-oriented or corporate action in everyday life is as necessary to prevent states of emergency as much as to cope with them. Further, Pratt sometimes pointedly neglects to compartmentalize crisis behaviour from ordinary duties, and thus writes as if society-centred behaviour were no more than should be expected at any time from any man. Such is clearly the message of the concluding passage of *The Roosevelt and the Antinoe*, where both the mundane and the heroic are merely parts of the 'day's work.'

> The nation gave its thanks on board; and she [the *Roosevelt*],
> Soon ready for completion of her run,
> Swung out the sound, with her day's work well done,
> And in an hour was on the Channel sea.

One might conclude from Pratt's selection and treatment of subjects that to him society always lives under threat of imminent crisis.

E. J. Pratt is a committed and somewhat uncritical spokesman for the values of industrial man. He has frequently been acknowledged as a humanist. To be more specific, Pratt is a Pelagian liberal, not only casting out original sin on a torrent of words from his "truant" but continually presenting both the machinery of technology and the machinery of social organization as man's best way to salvation. Just as human muscle successfully supplants the priest's prayers in *The Roosevelt and the Antinoe*, submarines, locomotives, and convoys supplant the early mystery behind "the iron door," and the truant's brash optimism supplants the poet's early but frail humility. Pratt's own frequent use of the personal pronoun *we* spells out his position: Pratt typically presents himself as the voice of his society rather than as an individual man. The world of E. J. Pratt is a world where the individual voice, the lyric voice, is silent, where gangs, crews, religions, and nations succeed, and private men die. It is a world where ships outlive successive crews, where the CPR outlives the individuals who built it, where it is *dulce et decorum* to die for one's faith, *patria*, ship, or family of whales.

1970

---

1. *The Poetry of E. J. Pratt: A New Interpretation* (Toronto: Ryerson, 1956).
2. *Ten Canadian Poets* (Toronto: Grenwoods, 1958).
3. "Editor's Introduction," *The Collected Poems of E. J. Pratt,* 2nd ed. (Toronto: Macmillan, 1958).
4. "E. J. Pratt and Christianity," *Canadian Literature* 19, 1964, 21-32.
5. "Introduction," *Selected Poems of E. J. Pratt* (Toronto: Macmillan, 1968), p. xvi.
6. "Editor's Introduction," p. xvii.
7. *Ibid,* p. xviii.
8. "E. J. Pratt's Literary Reputation," *Canadian Literature* 19, 1964, 9.
9. "E. J. Pratt and his Critics," in R. L. McDougall (ed.), *Our Living Tradition* (Toronto: University of Toronto Press, 1959), pp. 123-47.
10. "Dunkirk," in Northrop Frye (ed.), *The Collected Poems of E. J. Pratt.*
11. *Ten Canadian Poets,* p. 177.
12. "E. J. Pratt and his Critics," p. 136.
13. "E. J. Pratt and Christianity," p. 24.
14. "Introduction," *Selected Poems of E. J. Pratt,* p. xv.
15. "Editor's Introduction," p. xvii.
16. *Ten Canadian Poets,* p. 169.
17. *Ibid.,* p. 167.
18. "E. J. Pratt and Christianity," p. 26-9.
19. *Ten Canadian Poets,* p. 166.
20. *Quintessence of Capitalism,* tr. M. Epstein (New York: Fertig, 1967 [1915]).
21. *Religion and the Rise of Capitalism* (New York: Peter Smith, 1926).
22. *The Mechanical Bride* (Boston: Beacon Press, 1951), p. 33.
23. "Editor's Introduction," p. xx.
24. "Introduction," p. xxiv.
25. "Introduction," p. xix.
26. *The Mechanical Bride,* p. 128.
27. "Editor's Introduction," p. xvii.

E.J. PRATT: RATIONALIST TECHNICIAN

Little has been written about E.J. Pratt's handling of language and poetic form. His earlier reviewers and critics (Brown, Pierce, Norwood, and Collin) noted mainly his "vivid rhetoric," "surge and swing," "muscular lines," "energy and clamour," plus the epic point of view of his narrative poems. Later critics (Sutherland, Dudek, Sharman, Frye, Buitenhuis, Smith) have become overwhelmingly preoccupied with the thematic implications of his work. Even Frye's recent comments on Pratt's use of the epic mode have been directed more toward explaining certain limitations in the intellectual content of the poetry than toward illuminating its craft.[1]

Only A.J.M. Smith has attempted any detailed examination of Pratt's imagery. Although he too is more concerned with implication or content than with technique, his few technical comments are illuminating. At one point he tells us, "The qualities of the writing are speed, tautness, objectivity, and sharpness."[2] At another, "This is the poetry of wit."[3] As most students of Canadian poetry know, wit, objectivity, tautness are all qualities Smith has sought in his own poetry, and he has tended to find them in the work of many poets he admires. In Pratt's case, however, I believe he is extremely close to the truth.

An examination of Pratt's work reveals that he shares Smith's concept of the poet as a detached, dispassionate observer, that he believes in the myth of poetic objectivity. He appears to view the universe as rationally ordered, and to see the poet's task as consciously imparting a similar order to the creative work. Above all, Pratt, like Smith, can be seen to stand outside rather than inside his poetic materials, shaping them through sensibility and intelligence, rationally confronting 'problems' of convention, language, and form.

Pratt's shorter poems readily betray these beliefs. They are nearly all fitted smoothly into received verse patterns. The point of view is that of the essayist or commentator.

> The snarl Neanderthal is worn
> Close to the smiling Aryan lips.
> The civil polish of the horn
> Gleams from our praying finger tips.
>
> ("From Stone to Steel")

> Let the mind rest awhile, lower the eyes,
> Relieve the spirit of its Faustian clamour:
> An atom holds more secrets than the skies,
> Be patient with the earth and do not cram her
>
> With seed beyond the wisdom of her soil.
>
> ("The Good Earth")

There is little sense of subjectivity in them, even when the pronouns 'I' and 'my' replace the usual 'we' and 'our.' The pronouncements are made as ones of fact rather than feeling.

> His [death's] medieval grace is gone—
> Gone with the flame of the capitals

And the leisure turn of the thumb
Leafing the manuscripts.

("Come Away Death")

A number of these 'essay' poems are made to appear 'poetic' through ornamentation with imagery and metaphor.

Where do you bank such fires as can transmute
This granite-fact intransigence of life,
Such proud irenic faith as can refute
The upstart logic of this world of strife—

("The Mystic")

The imagery here is not endemic to the thought; it is applied arbitrarily by an authoritarian craftsman deliberately forging a specific effect. In some 'essay' poems, such as "The Baritone," a portrait of Adolf Hitler, Pratt creates elaborate analogies which provide a synthetic interpretive framework for the burden of the work. The result is clearly a poetry of the performing intelligence, of wit; it presents what is technically propaganda— subjectivity masquerading as objectivity.

He ascended the rostrum after the fashion of the Caesars:
His arm, a baton raised oblique,
Answering the salute of the thunder,
Imposed a silence on the Square.
For three hours
A wind-theme swept his larngeal reeds,
Pounded on the diaphragm of a microphone,
Entered, veered, ran round a coil,
Emerged, to storm the passes of the ether,
Until, impinging on a hundred million ear-drums,
It grew into the fugue of Europe.

Such decorative and argumentative use of metaphor also becomes one of the principal devices of the long narratives.

A few of these short poems achieve the economy, the impersonality, and the fascination with pattern of Smith himself—notably "The Shark," "The Drag Irons," and "Frost"— although in most of them lapses into conventional abstractions and rhetorical syntax give a most uneconomical appearance. Nevertheless, even these lapses betray a form of rationalism. The rhetoric is another sort of received form, the superimposing of an intellectualized structure on reality in the faith that such a structure will fit. The abstractions show a mind convinced of the objective reality of classification and generalization, a belief important to a poet who also writes epic narratives. In the epic such formulaic classification ("Hector of the shining helm") and abstraction ("*eorlic ellen*") allow for quick identification by the poet and instant recognition by the reader, so that both can pursue the narrative line without interruption by literary ambiguity. In Pratt's early lyrics they suggest only a sentimental belief in a regularized universe.

> Here the tides flow,
> ....
> ...with a lusty stroke of life
> ....
> That they might run
> Within the sluices of men's hearts,
> Leap under throb of pulse and nerve,
> And teach the sea's strong voice
> To learn the harmonies of new floods,
> The peal of cataract.
>
> ("Newfoundland")

Beneath the facade of cliché, metaphor, and rhetoric are certain large assumptions: that life is struggle ("lusty stroke"), that man is mechanical ("the sluices of men's hearts"), that the universe is possessed of increasing order ("to learn the harmonies of new floods").

The fact that many of Pratt's "lyrics" are actually short narrative poems again points out his rationalist stance. There are two approaches possible in the narrative: the subjective, in which the narrator can be within the story (*The Seafarer, The Rime of the Ancient Mariner,* or in prose (Richardson's archtypical *Pamela*), or the objective, in which he is excluded from it (*Beowulf, The Rape of Lucrece, The Rape of the Lock,* or Fielding's equally archtypical *Tom Jones*). Of all of Pratt's narratives only "The Iron Door" is of the former type, and even in it Pratt casts himself as a passive observer and focusses the narration on what happens before him rather than on what happens within him. The remainder of Pratt's narratives are of the objective kind, that in which the writer stands apart from his materials and in which he aspires toward Smith's ideals of impersonality and detachment. These narratives, like all of Pratt's shorter poetry, have very little explicit emotional content. There are no intimate relationships between characters, just as there are no expressions of intimate emotion in the lyrics. These characters are viewed from a distance, given identity only by their roles in the plot—a hero dog, an anonymous life-saver, a recalcitrant "truant." All become generic—the dog standing for its "breed," the truant for mankind.

It is not surprising that when attempting longer poems Pratt turned to the epic mode. In longer poetry the epic is the natural correlative to the impersonal lyric. The epic poet is totally detached from the story he is telling. He deals with it from a godlike stance—impersonally, making little attempt to involve the reader emotionally with its characters. The plot of the poem (comparable to the "pattern" of the lyric) is more important than its characters. The latter, in fact, are usually kept from having any large personal significance by a studied avoidance of psychological verisimilitude in their characterizations. They are viewed externally, superficially, and identified usually by formulaic, synecdochic, or metonymic tags ("Apollo of the silver bow"; "Diomede of the great war cry"). Or they are characterized by their birth and genealogy, the process involving that essential of rationalism, deductive logic.

In the epic, the myth of objectivity which possesses the impersonal lyricist is joined by the myth of omniscience: the poet must appear to know the story in its *absolute* form. The poet becomes an authority, responsible for his culture's history and obligated to maintain at least a pose of infallibility. The epic world is orderly and one-dimensional; it is conscious of few enigmas about its own character. It is rationalist to the point of believing that men are identifiable by tags and banners, that there is only one story implied by any one event, and above all, that this story is knowable by man. The fact that the most that any so-called 'objective' writer can achieve is subjectivity in the guise of objectivity is simply overlooked.

Two of Pratt's first three long narrative poems are mock-epic (*The Witches' Brew* and "The Great Feud"); the third ("The Cachalot") has a number of mock-epic elements. The mock-epic is even further removed from objective reality than the epic itself. As in the epic, its conventions are fixed and dominant, and bear no necessary relationship to the actual materials of the poem, but outside the conventions the poet is free to manipulate the materials into whatever shape best serves his personal and formal conceptions. The form requires no material, historical, or psychological realities. It is witty, fanciful, wilful, and synthetic. It possesses a reality fabricated in the human mind as opposed to a reality discovered in the circumstantial world. Described phenomenologically, the mock-epic offers a forged consciousness.

In each case Pratt presents reportorially scenes no human could observe—"The Great Feud" is set in the Pleiocene; *The Witches' Brew* and "The Cachalot" are set for the most part underwater. The reportorial mode is total. Despite "The Great Feud" being subtitled "A Dream of a Pleiocene Armageddon," neither it nor its companions contain any suggestion of authentic dream consciousness. The octosyllabics are terse, direct, mechanically rhythmic. The point of view is clearly objective.

> And thus it was throughout the whole
> Sea-range of the Australian zone
> The fear of racial doom was thrown
> Heavily upon the piscine soul.

A futile anger like a curse
Only made confusion worse.

("The Great Feud")

The imagery of these poems is the imagery of the inventive intelligence:

The bellows of his lungs might sail
A herring-skiff — such was the gale
Along the wind-pipe; and so large
The lymph-flow of his active liver
One might believe a fair-sized barge
Could navigate along the river;

("The Cachalot")

As long as Pratt is dealing with mythological creatures and arbitrary plots, and a deliberately superficial poetic mode, his manipulativeness can be delighting despite the resultant inconsequentiality. But in the documentary narratives Pratt's synthesizing habits are more troublesome. Their subjects are historical events; their agents are individual human beings with separate and complex identities which cannot be summed up in a deft image or a clever analogy.

Pratt appears to have done considerable research on the events of all these documentary narratives. Carl Klinck tells of Pratt's sailing on a Canadian destroyer in preparation for writing *Behind the Log.*[4] A number of sources, including Klinck and Dorothy Livesay,[5] report his spending at least several days aboard the United States Lines' *Roosevelt* before beginning *The Roosevelt and the Antinoe.* Klinck remarks that "he examined, with the technique of a detective, every deck, every log and barometric reading, and every person available where the liner docked in New York."[6] *Brébeuf and his Brethren* is based on the thirty-volume *Jesuit Relations; Towards the Last Spike* on newspaper and other records of the CPR's construction. In all this research Pratt seems to have been prepossessed with the material and technical aspects of his subjects. Northrop Frye recounts:

> In search of a monosyllable that would convey the hardness of rock, he ransacked a department of geology until he extracted the word "schist." While he was working on *Behind the Log*, anyone in a naval uniform he met would be backed into a corner and forced to reveal what he knew (or, more frequently, did not know) about the anatomy of a ship.[7]

Pratt shows no corresponding interest in non-quantifiable or non-factual information. The only reality which interests him is the knowable one—that of miles, tonnage, names, quotations, that which can be weighted, cited, documented, or otherwise rationalized. There is no mystery or ambiguity in these documentary narratives. "This strangely reasonable poet," as Klinck terms him,[8] writes as if personality can be summarized in a few phrases, moral qualities in a genealogical metaphor, motivation in a single analogy. His research into his characters appears to stop on the threshold—with, in the case of Captain Smith of the *Titanic*, a list of ships commanded, misadventures encountered, and commands issued. Material reality is assumed to contain, if not be, the whole.

The Titanic and *Towards the Last Spike* are excellent examples of Pratt's rationalist method in action. In each case the point of view is that of the detached, omniscient observer. In *The Titanic* he ranges throughout and around the ship, seeing the birth of the iceberg, knowing the contents of the ship's hold, overhearing conversations in the saloon, witnessing physical combat in the gymnasium, a poker game in a lounge, the officers' activities on the bridge. In *Towards the Last Spike* he pretends to oversee Parliament, the construction sites, John A. Macdonald's thoughts, William Van Horne's dreams. The poet's private responses to these various events are concealed. In actual fact the majority of these events have been fabricated by the poet and passed off as actual. Klinck's account of Pratt's "reasoning concerning the poker game in The Titanic"[9] makes clear the shrewd calculations involved in such a fabricating process. Pratt's rule seems to be that if an event is not totally knowable (and no event is), one must fake total knowledge. The existence of ignorance, ambiguity, or mystery is not to be admitted.

In both works Pratt's diction reinforces the overwhelming tone of confidence established by the omniscient point of view. The standard Pratt theme that nothing need be impossible to reasoning man is paralleled by an implicit assumption that nothing need be impossible to the careful poet. He can appear to know his subject absolutely. Research can give his diction two certainties: concrete detail and numerical exactitude. Invention can give it a third: dogmatic metaphor. The poet who can witness every event on a ship sinking ten years in the past is thus also one who need only declare a modifier or announce a metaphor to have these become arbitrarily, through his own authority, 'true.' This boldness of diction, metaphor, and analogy was suitable to the crafted gaiety of the mock-epics, and inspired his early critics to those comments about "infinite gusto," "boisterous writing," "energy and clamour." But in later poems such as *Towards the Last Spike*, where the reader can use his own experience of literal reality as a partial check on the fitness of the poet's figures, this temerity can lead to the inappropriate impression of extravagance and whimsy.

The most obvious characteristic of the diction of both these poems is that it is overwhelmingly specific—an important quality for a poet in creating the impression that he is totally in control of the substance of his narrative. Pratt's research has been scrupulous in gathering together the physical trappings of his subject: the *Titanic's* "tungsten chandeliers," "Chinese lanterns," "columned smoke," "burnished tile," "fiddleys," "bunkers," and "boiler rooms"; the CPR's origin in "rolling mills" and the saws that shaped "poles and sleepers," its prairie roadbed of "black alluvial mould," its "shovel gangs," "spiking gangs," "fish plates," and "double jacks." Where his research could not have sufficed, he has synthesized details and presented them as document. In *The Titanic* the wrestling holds and boxing blows demonstrated in the gymnasium ("Russian Hammerlock," "Polish scissors," "German crotch," "left hook," "right uppercut which Jeffries took from Johnson") are probably of this kind; the numerous passages of dialogue undoubtedly are. In *Towards the Last Spike* the thoughts attributed to George Stephen, the passage telling of Van Horne's scraping at a frosty window with his jackknife, the passage in which Macdonald seizes a telescope, and the passage beginning "Van Horne took off/His Coat" appear of dubious authenticity. A historian could probably find many more.

The second important characteristic of Pratt's diction in these poems is that it is consistently enumerating—again a characteristic which helps the poet toward a tone of confidence and knowledgeability. We are told that the *Titanic's* funnels have "thirty feet of bore," that her length is "from gudgeon to the stem nine hundred feet," that her engineering staff number "thirty-five," that her captain has "thirty years of service," that she has "seven decks of steel," "three electric lifts," that her tonnage is "sixty thousand tons of sheer flotation," "fifty thousand gross." Just before the collision, Pratt writes,

> The ocean sinuous, half-past eleven;
> A silence broken only by the seven
> Bells and the look-out calls, the log-book showing
> Knots forty-five within two hours...

When the ship is sinking, we are told that number three boat, with "sixty-five capacity," is launched with only twenty-four aboard, that number one, "her space is forty," is launched with only twelve, that number ten is launched with a "load of sixty" who collectively weigh "four tons" and takes "sixty seconds of descent" from davits to water.

In *Towards the Last Spike* Pratt uses diction of a similar numerical specificity. Dollars, miles, the duration of speeches, the length of work shifts, the age of rocks, the thickness of strata are all given precise quantity or measure. Although Macdonald, Van Horne, Smith, and Stephen, the major figures of the poem, are cast as romantic visionaries who make their dreams dominate the obstinate weights and dimensions of material reality, it is to a large extent by relying himself on these weights and measures that Pratt attempts to make both dream and dreamer tangible to his readers. Thus Macdonald and his fellow railway builders appear to succeed despite measurable reality; Pratt as poet succeeds because of it.

Even when attempting to characterize these dreamers directly, Pratt resorts to a rationalizing technique: metaphor— which is the third and most outstanding characteristic of his diction. Metaphor in Pratt's work tends to be a restricting device. The subject of the metaphor is compared to a term or set of terms either less complex than the subject itself, or possessing a complexity irrelevant to the subject. The effect is to simplify or rationalize the subject, to make it appear definable and comprehensible when it has been neither defined nor comprehended. The subject is presented as if 'dealt with' when in fact its own particularity and individuality have been avoided.

The most striking example of Pratt's presenting metaphoric whimsey in the guise of historic understanding is the well-known "oatmeal" passage of *Towards the Last Spike*—one of several metaphors by which the poet pretends to understand his CPR dreamers.

> Oatmeal was in their blood and in their names.
> Thrift was the title of their catechism.
> It governed all things but their mess of porridge
> Which, when it struck the hydrochloric acid
> With treacle and skim-milk, became a mash.
> Entering the duodenum, it broke up
> Into amino acids: then the liver
> Took on its natural job as carpenter:
> Foreheads grew into cliffs, jaws into juts.
> The meal, so changed, engaged the follicles:
> Eyebrows came out as gorse, the beards as thistles,
> And the chest-hair the fell of Grampian rams.
> It stretched and vulcanized the human span:
> Nonagenarians worked and thrived upon it.
> Out of such chemistry run through by genes,
> The food released its fearsome racial products:—
> The power to strike a bargain like a foe,

> To win an argument upon a burr,
> Invest the language with a Bannockburn,
> Culloden or the warnings of Lochiel,
> Weave loyalties and rivalries in tartans,
> Present for the amazement of the world
> Kilts and the civilized barbaric Fling,
> And pipes which, when they acted on the mash,
> Fermented Lullabies to *Scots wha hae.*

Critics may delight in the wit of such a passage, yet it remains despite all its intrinsic qualities a sentimental and spurious treatment of its subject. Elsewhere Macdonald is metaphorically portrayed as the merchant wooer of British Columbia, which is in turn portrayed as an aging maiden. Van Horne is usually painted as a military conqueror, although also variously compared to a bobcat, Paul Bunyan, and the Flying Dutchman. Donald Smith is compared to "Moses, Marco-Polo, Paracelsus," in addition to being characterized as: "A Scot with smoke of peat fire on his breath—/Smith? Yes: but christened Donald Alexander/And loined through issue from the Grants and Stuarts."

All such metaphorical and genealogical characterizations are merely referential to the reality of the man characterized. They substitute a rational concept in the place of that more difficult thing, actuality. The characterizations of *The Titanic* are similarly oversimplified by the use of metaphor. The various financiers aboard are summed up as "Gray-templed Caesars of the world's Exchange." A young boy who surrenders his place in a lifeboat is said to pile "The inches on his stature as he gave/ Place to a Magyar woman and her child."

The immigrants aboard are given a particularly prejudicial image by Pratt's use of metaphor: "In steerage—seven hundred immigrants!/ Smith thought of panic clutching at their throats,/And feared that Balkan scramble for the boats." In each case the subject has been unfairly treated; the metaphor has said far less than needed to be said while pretending to say all.

All of these cases of characterizing metaphor can be loosely grouped with a larger species of metaphor in Pratt: interpretive metaphor. In the narrative poems such metaphor is Pratt's usual way of dealing with difficult aspects of actuality. We find such a metaphor at the beginning of *Brébeuf:*

> The winds of God were blowing over France,
>
> ....
>
> The air was charged with song beyond the range
> Of larks, with wings beyond the stretch of eagles.
> Skylines unknown to maps broke from the mists
> And there was laughter on the seas.

Here the simplifying images of soaring nature enable Pratt to avoid dealing directly with the potentially troublesome topic of religious inspiration. *Towards the Last Spike* contains the most spectacular such metaphor in his work: the reptile image he gives to the Laurentian Shield. Pratt appears to become more fascinated with this metaphor than he is with the actual building of the railroad. As a result the reader is shown very little of this part of the railroad's construction. Instead he reads of a reptile sleeping, folding, curling, drowsing, and stirring; reads of its "rock and mineral mattress," its "spotty carboniferous hair," its "scales," its "drowsing coils," its "higher vertebrae," its "deep layers and arteries," its "table-clothes of sphagnum moss," its "counterpane of leather-leaf and slime." Most important, he never does see this section of the railroad completed, or learn how Van Horne ovecomes the final barrier of muskeg. The metaphor causes Pratt to evade the literal building. Despite his usual show of numbers and particulars—shovels, pick-axes, black powder, abutments, trestles, "three engines," "seven tracks"—he has in fact substituted an interpretive rationalization in the place of the actual event. The struggle between the lizard and man may be Pratt's interpretation of the event, but it is not, as Pratt pretends, objectively the event. The event was both the metaphor and much more.

What is typical of this metaphor is that it is tangential to actuality. It represents a movement by the poet away from the matter. Pratt is thus enabled to create his own Van Horne, his own Macdonald, or his own Captain Smith under the cover of presenting historical fact. Further, the non-metaphoric aspects of his diction, its enumerating and specifying qualities, as well as providing the poet with a non-mysterious and intelligible working surface, serve to mask his metaphoric caprices with a veneer of factuality.

Metaphor is such a ubiquitous property of Pratt's diction that throughout his work it appears as an entrenched writing habit. Many of these metaphors are of the casual or colloquial sort that one is hardly aware of when writing or reading. "Water was swirling up the slanted floor/Around the chair and sucking at his feet" (*The Titanic*).

More developed kinds appear as habitual means in Pratt for avoiding the delineation of human personality. Military metaphors are especially frequent. Passengers on the *Titanic* are said to rally from flight "as if [stiffened by] the rattle of a drum." Her diners mass before the salon "like storm troops before a citadel." In *Towards the Last Spike* almost every participant is characterized at some time in military terms.

> But here this was a theme less vulnerable
> To fire, Macdonald thought, to Blake's gunfire,
> And yet....
>
> Here he [Van Horne] could clap the future on the shoulder
> And order Fate about as his lieutenant....
>
> The men were fighting foes which had themselves
> Waged elemental civil war....
>
> Into this scrimmage came the fighting men....
>
> ...their weapons were their hands
> And backs, pickaxes, shovels, hammers, drills,
> And dynamite....

Still other metaphors appear to be attempts to make physical reality more colourful and interesting than it might otherwise appear. The reptile metaphor for the Laurentian Shield certainly appears touched by this motive. In the following passage in which Macdonald reflects on the task of building the CPR, several metaphors appear chiefly decorative:

> But this would be a longer tug
> Of war which needed for his team thick wrists
> And calloused fingers, heavy heels to dig
> Into the earth and hold—men with bull's beef
> Upon their ribs. Had he himself the wind,
> The anchor-waist to peg at the rope's end?
> 'Twas had [*sic*] enough to have these questions hit
> The waking mind: 'twas much worse when he dozed;
> For goblins had a way of pinching him,
> Slapping a nightmare on to dwindling snoozes.

Occasionally Pratt's fondness for such decoration causes the metaphors to become badly mixed. Here the *Titanic's* adversary iceberg is transmogrified from calf, to ship, to island within six lines.

> Calved from a galcier near Godhaven coast,
> It left the fiord from the sea—a host
> Of white flotillas gathering in its wake,
> And joined by fragments from a Behring floe,
> Had circumnavigated it to make
> It centre of an archipelago.

Later a *Titanic* distress rocket is an arrow, a spire, and a parasol within three.

> An arrow of fire,
> A fourth sped toward the sky, its bursting spire
> Topping the foremast like a parasol
> With fringe of fuschia,...

In these instances Pratt's inventiveness has overreached itself. Had he confined himself to perceptual responses to actuality, no such confusion could have occurred. Instead, by responding intellectually, he departs from actuality's inherent order, and enters the separate world of human invention—a world which is not only separate and arbitrary but fallible.

I believe it unquestionable that throughout his career, in both lyrics and narratives, Pratt was an impersonal, manipulative, synthesizing, rationalist craftsman. He is certainly not an anomaly in Canadian poetry, and not, as Earle Birney once suggested, "old-fashioned."[10] He is squarely in the cosmopolitan-traditionalist stream of A.J.M. Smith, Robert Finch, P.K. Page, James Reaney, Jay Macpherson, and Eli Mandel—a stream guarded since the fifties by the criticism of Northrop Frye. It should be seen as no accident that among the most enthusiastic of Pratt's later commentators have been Reaney, Smith, and Frye. Reaney's defence of Pratt's narrative methods is a simple statement of a poet's authority and license—"The poet...can take imaginative leaps that the historian does not have to take." "The poet is allowed a view of another reality."[11] Of course a poet can do these things, but not, as Pratt does, in order to pass such leaps and views off as objective fact. Later, Reaney praises Pratt for "purposeful distortions"[12] of history, for exaggerating it "sky high,"[13] for creating scenes which "ring true poetically."[14] All these are praises of the fabricating consciousness which superimposes its own structure on reality and decorates that reality with synthesized effects.

There is, it should be noted, a remarkable congruity between Pratt's themes and his techniques. As I have argued in an earlier article, he is throughout his work an apologist for the Pelagian view of man—that view in which mankind can, by social co-operation, discipline, vigilance, the application of reason, and the suppression of individualism, overcome any difficulty. That is, corporate man can be the rationalist craftsman of his own destiny. In his writing Pratt adopts the point of view of the impersonal spokesman for mankind, adopts group values, and writes social epics. He represses overt statements of individual sensibility, masking these as objective statements of fact.

In technique he regards his materials as impersonally as the Pelagian regards the universe—as things to be specified, counted, or altered as the intellect requires. As a result, more so than the work of any other Canadian poet, Pratt's poetry becomes dedicated to the celebration of human ingenuity and craftsmanship. Its themes honour rationalist hopes, its form exemplifies rationalist methodologies. Even its limitations are faithful to the character of the Pelagian/humanist dream.

---

1. "Silence in the Sea," in David G. Pitt (ed.), *E. J. Pratt* (Toronto: Ryerson, 1969), pp. 124-138.

2. "Some Poems of E. J. Pratt: Aspects of Imagery and Theme," in Pitt (ed.), *E. J. Pratt*, p. 142.

3. p. 148.

4. Henry W. Wells and Carl F. Klinck, *Edwin J. Pratt* (Toronto: Ryerson, 1947), p. 52.

5. "The Documentary Poem: A Canadian Genre," in Eli Mandel (ed.), *Contexts of Canadian Criticism* (Chicago: University of Chicago Press, 1971), p. 278.

6. *Edwin J. Pratt*, p. 52.

7. "Editor's Introduction," *The Collected Poems of E. J. Pratt*, 2nd ed. (Toronto: Macmillan, 1958), pp. xvi-xvii.

8. *Edwin J. Pratt*, p. 52.

9. p. 46.

10. "E. J. Pratt and His Critics," in A.J.M. Smith (ed.), *Masks of Poetry* (Toronto: McClelland and Stewart, 1962), p. 94.

11. "Towards the Last Spike: The Treatment of a Western Subject," in Pitt (ed.), *E. J. Pratt*, p. 76.

12. p. 78.

13. p. 77.

14. p. 79.

GWENDOLYN MACEWEN: THE SECRET OF ALCHEMY

In Gwendolyn MacEwen's second novel, *King of Egypt, King of Dreams* (1971), the central character, the 14th century B.C. King Akhenaton, is obsessed by a desire to articulate the ineffable. "It was a long time before he could successfully explain the inexplicable or speak the unspeakable. The very nature of his vision was such that mere words could not convey it" (*KEKD*, 41). The task involves not only language but perception and apprehension; what is to be described must first be found, seen, and understood. "'You mean,' he asked, 'the form which *contains* Ra like a vessel containing fluid? The circle which *surrounds* the god but is not in itself the god...?'" (*KEKD*, 40). To a great extent, Akhenaton's quest for both divine vision and articulation of this vision is also Gwendolyn MacEwen's. All of her writing to date has involved inquiry into the process by which mystical enlightenment can be gained—by which the bland phenomena of this world can be induced to reveal arcane knowledge. Her novels and short stories have all been centred on characters who have in some way sought to link the divine and the actual, to transform the mundane into the miraculous. Her poetry has continually celebrated such transformation, urged readers to attempt similar transformations, or attempted to reveal the process of visionary experience through the kinetics of the personal lyric. Much of both her poetry and her fiction has attempted to 'embody' divine truth in the way in which she evidently believes that the phenomena of this world contain, imply, or reveal it.

The precise nature of MacEwen's preoccupations was evident as early as her first novel, *Julian the Magician* (1963). Its epigraph was taken from the *Pistis Sophia*, a third-century A.D. Coptic manuscript; this epigraph, which predicts "the completion of all the completeness," placed the novel immediately within the tradition of the mystic quest to see divine and human nature as indissolubly united yet distinct, separate yet inseparable. Julian, the novel's main character, apprentices with the magician Kardin, whose chief pursuit is alchemy—the mediaeval study of transmuting metals, personalities, spirits, male and female, solar and lunar, fine and dross, into a single and transcending *res simplex*, usually symbolized in the divinity 'Mercurius.' Julian's personal sources include the Zohar, the Kabbalah, the writings of the Gnostics, Paracelsus, Albertus Magnus, and above all Jacob Boehme, whose godhead was simultaneously *nichts und alles*. Julian himself symbolizes the union of antinomies, being an illegitimate child fathered on a blonde girl by a dark gypsy lover, coming consequently to be an incongruously blond magician with dark gypsy eyes.

Early in this novel Julian comes to believe that his body is being taken over by Christ. Such an event would represent, of course, an interaction between the terrestrial and celestial realms—an accomplishment of the aims of the alchemical tradition which Julian's master, Kardin, had followed. It would also mark the return of a Christ who was himself *deus-homo*, an instance of the combining of the two realms. As Julian's sense of possession grows, he, the Christ within him, or the new transmuted being that is the two of them, cries out: "A-ha! Alpha and Omega! That mystery is I, and I am that mystery. I am Alpha and Omega, the duality of existence, the attainment of completeness ..." (*JM*, 18-19). Thus in Julian the terms of the epigraph—"the completion of all the completeness"— are apparently fulfilled. But Julian feels compelled by the 'Christ' within him to seek a further completion—the completion of a re-enactment of Christ's death. His diary (given as an appendix to the novel) suggests that Christ totally usurps Julian's consciousness and personally stage-manages the necessary happenings to bring about the crucifixion. But the main narrative which is told from the point of view of a variably omniscient narrator[1] leaves it ambiguous whether Julian is compelled by delusions of being Christ or whether he is indeed possessed by an alien psyche. The narrator's final comment is "we do not know" (*JM*, 151).

However, the similarity between Julian's story and what Carl Jung reports as one of the central goals of the alchemic devotee is striking.

> If the adept expresses his own self, the 'true man,' in his work, then, as the passage from the 'Aquarium sapientum' shows, he encounters the analogy of the true man—Christ—in new and direct form, and he recognizes in the transformation in which he himself is involved a similarity to the Passion. It is not an 'imitation of Christ' but its exact opposite: an assimilation of the Christ-image to his own self, which is the 'true man.' It is no longer an effort, an intentional straining after imitation, but rather an involuntary experience of the reality represented by the sacred legend.
>
> (*Mysterium Coniunctionis*, 349)

Julian's crucifixion is not an "imitation" of that of Christ's. He is tied, rather than nailed, to a makeshift cross that has been cut from a nearby tree and leaned against another tree for support. There are no thieves to accompany him to death. The resultant scene has as much similarity to the Hanged Man of the Tarot as to the passion on Calvary.

> Two men hoisted the magician and the cross. They propped it against a tree. Somehow they were disappointed—there really

> wasn't the least bit of excitement. The thing didn't even look dramatic. It looked just like a magician tied to a silly cross and propped against a tree. (*JM*, 103)

Further, if Julian's diary is correct, his experience of being Christ was an "involuntary experience," one which he was called to by the success of his magicianship but which he nevertheless resisted when its final and complete domination of his psyche was at hand. "I don't want to be divine," he tells Christ, but afterward yields, saying, "And suddenly it is good, it is like sleep, to give myself over to him... he asks only occupation, residence—and that I give." (*JM*, 140)

A parallel to Julian's life which the novel appears to invite is that of the life of Julian the Apostate, fourth-century A.D. Roman emperor. He too was the student of a magician, Maximus of Ephesus, and later devoted himself to Mithraism in much the same way that MacEwen's Julian devotes himself to the teachings of Paracelsus and Boehme. He resisted Christianity as energetically as the later Julian resists his occupation of Christ. His apocryphal last words, "Thou has conquered, O Galilean," uttered after suffering a Judas-like betrayal by a Persian nobleman and being mortally wounded at the head of his army, echo the last ones of Julian on capitulating his individuality to Christ: "You have control. You wear me well" (*JM*, 117). The force of this parallel is to suggest the timelessness of Christ's presence; his incarnation, his death, his resurrection are continually recurring. "Without time and location we cannot place his figure anywhere in history" (*JM*, 151).

King of Egypt, King of Dreams is technically a superior novel to its predecessor. The point of view does not suffer from the inconsistencies of the earlier work. The personality and vision of the central character are more fully and concretely sketched—possibly because, since he is a failed mystic, they are more amenable to verbal representation. Further, MacEwen has abandoned the annoying habit of overemphasizing the meaning of certain aspects of her work (in *Julian* each episode re-enacting Christ's life is prefaced by a 'realistic' retelling of the relevant Biblical event—ostensibly to show that the two events are co-present in time, if not timeless, but in the process creating numerous redundancies).

King Akhenaton is at first glance a very similar character to Julian. By birth he is considered half-human and half-divine —son of a mortal mother and, through his reputed father, Amenhotep III, of the god Amon. His childhood and adolescence are steeped in the theological lore of the Egyptian royal court, much as Julian's adolescence is dominated by the alchemist Kardin. But whereas Julian wished to be only a simple magician and never sought to embrace spiritual truth, Akhenaton constantly and consciously strives toward the divine. Late in the novel the reader learns some ironic facts behind his quest. Akhenaton is not Amenhotep's son, and thus not a half-divine child of Amon. His father is his mother's brother, It Neter Ay, the worldly general of the Pharoah's cavalry. Apparently Akhenaton is not spiritually equipped for enlightenment; his only course is the rational quest ("You mean the form which *contains* Ra?" [*KEKD*, 40]) which by its very means is antithetical to spiritual success.

Instead of bringing him to a vision which truly unites the physical and the divine, Akhenaton's quest moves him closer to the divine only by alienating him from the earthly. He can transcend but not transmute; his religious preoccupations take him away from the day-to-day affairs of state. His successful building of a new and "pure" capital city serves mainly to alienate him from the everyday reality of the Egyptian nation. He can apprehend the divine, yet not in any way return the apprehension to the terrestrial world. His attempts to define the godhead result in its becoming not only more remote to him ("the more he attempted to simplify the Teaching the more murky his meaning became") but more and more distant to the mundane lives of his people.

> ...the people could only understand personal gods, friendly beings they could speak to, clutch to their breasts, wear about their necks. But the supreme Aton was remote to them, fearful and

> inaccessible in his majesty. They couldn't accustom themselves to the 'royal god' in any of his forms. They couldn't conquer their terrible awe of Ra; he was lord and protector of all who lived—but he was not human, not even animal. Not close, but huge and remote. (*KEKD*, 128)

The lesson of the alchemists that the divine is attained only through its union with the material—through the blending of light and dark, good and evil, sun and moon—has been lost to Akhenaton. Symbolic of his one-sidedness is the fact that although he feels compelled to worship and experience continually the rays of Aton the sun-god, he cannot endure Aton's other—the moon and her accompanying darkness. His exasperated father-in-law, It Neter Ay, cries out to him one evening:

> Who has ever seen you outside at night? No one. Ra is in the underworld battling the demons of the darkness. Some say you fear blindness but I know it is more than that! Why have you avoided moonlight for so many years, why do you fear the dark? Speak! (*KEKD*, 94)

The consequences of Akhenaton's obsession with the sun and its light at the expense of the realms of darkness and corporeality is paradoxically that his land must live in darkness. Akhenaton cannot bring light to the darkness as a sun-king or a Christ is obliged to do. His father-in-law comments:

> The land lived in a kind of eclipse when he reigned, though he sang day and night to the sun. But it was a shadow, so black that only a great form standing behind a great light might have cast it, and even now its dark fingers stretch across the floor and touch my sandals. (*KEKD*, 231)

It is an ancient wisdom that the sun contains its other, the *sol niger*, that without light there can be no shadow and no darkness. Akhenaton fails to see this, until finally the neglected night herself defeats him. She afflicts him with blindness, she besets him with fever until he cries out "there is no more light." Delirious, he runs out under the full moon, disguised as his other, a woman, and wearing a white crown. He calls upon Ay, who is both his father-in-law and his natural father, "to right the balances," to kill him there in the moonlight (*KEKD*, 248). Afterward the jackals who both worship the moon and draw the boat of Ra tear apart his corpse. It Neter Ay relates the moral to be drawn from the Pharoah's life:

> It is a lie to assume there is only light, only goodness . . . the holy and the obscene exist side by side; beneath Heaven is *Duat*, and beneath the bright heart of a man is the dark underworld of his soul. (*KEKD*, 235)

Curiously, Ay becomes the true adept of *King of Egypt, King of Dreams*. He is the only character to come to the insight represented in the above passage. He completes the ritual of Akhenaton's death; in slaying him he appears simultaneously aware of both the deed's earthly and celestial ramifications. "'My Sun Akhenaton!' I cried, and I lunged forward with my knife " (*KEKD*, 249). Though considered an "Unbeliever" by Akhenaton, he seems to possess the true paradoxical sense of the unity of the material and the divine requisite for spiritual insight. "Isn't the greatest adoration born of the greatest doubt?" he asks. "Are not Priest and Unbeliever, finally, of the same spirit?" (*KEKD*, 253)

MacEwen's most recent fiction, *Noman* (1972), continues to deal with either failed mystics such as Akhenaton or unwittingly successful ones such as Julian and It Neter Ay. The central and uniting symbol of this collection of stories is W. L. Mackenzie King's "Kingsmere"; its carefully fabricated ruins both represent a sentimental and overly conscious striving for the mystic light and paradoxically, provide for the characters of the title story "Noman" an archway into the real. The opening story of the collection, "House of the Whale," tells of a

Haida Indian, Lucas George, who discovers himself to be reliving a tribal myth when he attempts to make a life for himself in Toronto. "Fire" presents a young couple whose fascination with a new fireplace suddenly moves them to an illusion of primeval, ice-threatened survival and to a frenzied potlatch-burning of her possessions in order to keep the life-giving flames alive. In "The Oarsman and the Seamstress," a young woman attempts to blend waking reality with her imagined images of her lover's sleeping dream. In "Snow" the efforts of a south-European immigrant to Toronto to wed his Mediterranean body to the Canadian snows which have dazzled and entranced him since his arrival leads to his death—incongruously nude and smiling in a snowdrift. All these stories are tales of ritual sacrifice, of symbolic or ritual death, of accidental mystic illumination placed in convincingly concrete and contemporary Canadian settings.

The title story, "Noman," which concludes the collection, has its actual beginning in an earlier story, "Day of the Twelve Princes." Here, somewhere in Ontario in 1954, a fourteen-year-old boy, Samuel (this name translates from the Hebrew as "his name is god") scours the dreary phenomenal world for spiritual enlightenment. There is a tree branch he worships from an attic window "at an appointed time each afternoon when the sun touched it tentatively, from the left."

> And the sun ran its fingers along the body of the branch, tracing, exploring, transforming it into a narrow golden bow, a weapon of pure fire, unstrung, divorced from the tree. And Samuel thought: Therefore this fire is also mine and the power that goes with it. (*N*, 26)

At a circus he steals a large Arabian horse and rides it to its exhaustion, lying down beside it in the grass, saying "I am the earth, the turf, the trees, the fire in the Arab's body" (*N*, 37).

Samuel, we learn later in Part II of "Noman," is the adolescent Noman. He has worked in a circus as a clown and as an escape artist, he has worked as a dancer, and he has at some time become wealthy.

He is now in the company of 'Kali,' his mistress whom he has thus nick-named, and of 'Jubelas' and 'Omphale,' a married but childless couple to whom he has also given names. Jubelas, who narrates Part I, seems so named because he is a shallow-minded enthusiast who finds almost anything to be as "fascinating" as the film *Lawrence of Arabia*. Omphale, in mythology the Lydian Cybele and mother of the gods, is appropriately maternal in appearance and mannerism, and at one point dreams "she had given miraculous birth to Noman in the middle of Bay Street after stars and planets had rolled around in her belly" (*N*, 97). Kali, in Hindu mythology the wife of the dancing Siva, is a logical name for a dancer's consort, and in Part II, which she narrates, she obligingly completes the expected equation: "I saw Noman as Siva . . ." (*N*, 109).

Noman clearly fulfills in the story the role of Siva, the creative destroyer. When Kali meets him he is working on the demolition of an old Toronto bank. Some time after, in order to resolve a disagreement with Kali, he smashes a statue of a Caananite goddess against his apartment wall. Under his influence Jubelas destroys a juke-box and he and Omphale embark on an orgy of shoplifting. When Noman and Kali finally make love, she reports:

> We emerged from the night beaten and bruised, as if we'd come out of a den of lions, or had become gladiators, bloody and victorious after the games. My loins were broken; armies had marched over them and crushed them into sand. (*N*, 114)

Late in the story Kali decides that Noman must appear to die in order to be free of Jubelas and Omphale. With her help, Noman convincingly feigns a bloody death, and is thus able to "rise again" above the mundane and the motherly to seek a new "future." Significantly, he begins this search by making the fraudulent ruins of Mackenzie King's Kingsmere serve as the gateway to the authentic.

> 'Noman, what are we *doing* here?' I cried. 'Whose past have we stolen? Into whose future are we moving?'

> And he (swiftly removing his clothes) called back to me—
> 'Why our own, of course!'
> And blithely stepped, stark naked, through the arch. (*N*, 120)

MacEwen appears to want us to see Noman and Kali as a contemporary Siva and Kali, as contemporary iconoclasts and innovators whose destruction of the Canadian past paradoxically creates the possibility of a future. In their sexual embrace they echo that of Siva and Kali (incarnate as Parvati/Shakti) which combines male and female, destruction and love, to form Siva's full reality—a paradoxical reality preserved in Hindu folklore in the interlocking lingam-yoni symbol. In turn, that embrace echoes the alchemists' 'royal marriage' of energy and love.

Siva encompasses many of the characters and events of the other stories in the collection. In his consuming 'fire' aspect he is the god of the story by that name. His is the Mediterranean heat which tries disasterously in "Snow" to unite with the Canadian winter. His role in disdaining the present commercial reality of Toronto repeats in part the plot of "House of the Whale." As Siva, Noman subsumes the Haida myth's Gunarh, finding not only his "psyche" but the future which Lucas George is denied. Siva also encompasses the heroes of MacEwen's novels. In joining himself with Kali/Parvati/Shakti he combines fire and love in the same way that Julian's Christ does in combining the Holy Ghost and the Virgin Mary; in passing through Kingsmere's ruins in order to approach new possibility, he accomplishes a union of the obscene and the holy similar to that recommended by It Neter Ay, MacEwen's spokesman in *King of Egypt, King of Dreams*.

The most outstanding technical feature of these novels and stories is that the various myths seldom appear merely superimposed on the action. The leading characters—Akhenaton, It Neter Ay, Julian, Noman, Kali—are all convincingly drawn figures, with plausible motivations and realistic and colloquial dialogue. The artistic effort is not one of stories contrived to parallel myths, but of characters who discover themselves reliving myth involuntarily and often unprofitably. Rather than the artifactual sense of myth conveyed in poetry by Macpherson's *The Boatman* or Reaney's *A Suit of Nettles*, one finds here kinetic myth—myth alive and re-enacted in the spontaneous actions of real people. The alchemical paradox is achieved in that the "Word" becomes both flesh and fact. The mythic meanings appear implicit in MacEwen's fiction not because she has wanted them to be but because the actions she has recounted have required them.

The task of explaining "the inexplicable" and speaking the "unspeakable" that MacEwen's fiction carries out so well appears to be also the primary goal of her poetry. Three of the book titles invoke planetary bodies: *The Armies of the Moon* (1972) calling on Luna, *The Rising Fire* (1963) and *The Shadow Maker* (1969) naming Sol; the latter title calls forth numerous mystic opposites—sun and moon, the shadow-maker and the shadow, animus and anima. The title poem of *A Breakfast for Barbarians* (1966) asks "barbarians"—ostensibly those who can combine opposites to achieve unity—to reveal "their most unspeakable appetites," to "consume" their mysteries (*BB*, 1). Another poem in this collection is entitled "Black Alchemy" and relates the birth of Mercurius, the prime deity of the alchemical tradition, from out of the *aqua permanens* of the Mercurial Fountain,

> whose waves transmuted him
> from the hot metallic laughter
>
> Of their wake. He is neither metal nor water
> nor fluid nor solid, but born from the darkest
> paradox of his body are forms without terms
> and substances which seek their names in laughter. (*BB*, 40)

Two lines further the figure becomes Christ, "the second adam," and a stanza later is called "a dervish" who turns "in his dance" like Siva (*BB*, 40).

The dominant concepts of the poetry are all ones which are important to various of the mystics who inhabit MacEwen's fiction;

all deal with the nature of the arcane or "unspeakable" and the way to its apprehension. Repeatedly the poetry tells us that the mythic structure of reality is binary.

> We, caught on a split organ of chaos
> On the right half of a bisected goddess
> wonder why moon pulls sea on a silver string,
> why earth will not leave the gold bondage of the sun,
> why all parts marry, all things couple in confusion (*RF*, 5)

Every part of creation has its other; she asks us "Can you lose the shadow which stalks the sun?" (*SM*, 14). Inside a "tame" and quiet city,

> O inside houses
> are wilder things—dynasties, wars,
> empires crumbling, chariots housed
> in halls, emperors in cupboards,
> queens and generals in beds,
> kingdoms rising and falling between the sheets. (*SM*, 35)

In this view "arguments . . . are hidden agreements" (*BB*, 19), "all times, all loves are one" (*SM*, 68), "the bear and the eagle/burn together" (*RF*, 37), and death "cleaves what it most loves" (*AM*, 24). "Without these shadows," she tells us, "I would be/in air one wave of ruinous light" (*SM*, 80).

Because of the binary structure of the cosmos, knowledge is discoverable primarily through inverse means.

> This land like a mirror turns you inward
> And you become a forest in a furtive lake:
> The dark pines of your mind reach downward,
> You dream in the green of your time,
> Your memory is a row of sinking pines. (*SM*, 50)

It can be attained in apparent madness, madness similar to that which led Julian to seek his own crucifixion or sent Akhenaton out into the night in search of moonlight, jackals and death. Sanity, on the other hand, can blind one's eyes to the divine fire. "I do not fear that I will go mad/but that I may not, and the shadows of my sanity/blacken out your burning;..." (*BB*, 42). Knowledge comes to those who seek sanity in insanity, intelligence in darkness, who seek the universe within themselves, who would find answers in the interrogative sign.

> ...the introverted eye looks inward
> to find the inward Eye looking out
> as finally, the astronaut swims
> through yellow yolks of total suns
> towards the ultimate inquiry—
> (even the darkness has
> a certain intelligence)
> and finds at the end of the universe
> not walls, but mirrors
> reflecting the question mark
> of his own face back in
> to study it ironically,
> like brothers, amazed
> at their own similarity. (*RF*, 12)

Says MacEwen in another context, "Only because my poems are lies do they earn the right to be truth" (*BB*, 26).

Illumination is also to be attained, as in the alchemical tradition, through the coupling of opposites.

> we are only complete when
>
> that image of me in you
> that image of you in me
> breaks, repairs itself. (*BB*, 3)

Throughout her poems the idea prevails that various opposites—light and darkness, predator and prey, man and woman, terrestrial and celestial—must be reconciled if human life is to achieve its true potential. Various symbols of such reconciliation are common in the poetry: Jekyll and Hyde (*BB*, 26), the astronaut (*BB*, 17), Sir James Frazer's 'Maimed King,' with one leg normal and the other deformed by his divine role and therefore useless in earthly life (*BB*, 27), Tiamut, the bisected goddess (*RF*, 5), the magician (*BB*, 36), the escape artist (*BB*, 37)—to point out only a few. The attempt to invoke the inverse in order to bring opposites together is perhaps clearest in two poems in *The Shadow Maker.* In the first, "Invocations," MacEwen announces that because the world so abounds in actual dangers and predatory beasts,

> ...I invoke you, red beast
> who moves in my blood,
> demon of my darker self,
> denizen who crawls in my deep want,
> white crow, black dove,
> eagle and vulture of my love,
> and you great buzzard of my dreams,
> I call you down
> ....
> to see those things I cannot use
> (the broken edges of the air,
> the flicker of forms before they occur). (*SM*, 6)

In the second, "Dream Two: The Beasts," we see her attempting to be the uniting link between two beasts both actual and symbolic:

> A big red tiger and a dog black as earth
> Hating each other and snarling and clawing,
> Each of them wanting to get to me first.
>
> The red one leapt forward and gazed at me long,
> Then leaned on my right side, heavy and warm;
> The dog followed after and leaned on my left
> And I felt as mighty as a coat-of-arms. (*SM*, 55)

A psychological reading of this dream poem would see the two beasts as MacEwen's unconscious and conscious selves, and the policeman who later intervenes saying "It's illegal to draw opposites together," as the Freudian superego. A reading in the Christian mystic tradition would see the poem as offering a "royal marriage" between solar red and lunar black, one opposed by the world of skeptical empiricism. A purely literary reading would find the two beasts symbolic of any two contraries potentially resolvable by love—"they forgot their hate in their love for me" (*SM*, 55)—and find the intervening policeman to represent the paralyzing force of public morality. In any reading, the poem advocates an effort to unite opposites in order to achieve "love" or harmony, an effort embraced by the Akhenaton of MacEwen's novel, by the early Coptic church, by the Gnostics, by Paracelsus, by Boehme, by the alchemists, by Noman, and by Christ in *Julian the Magician*.

The goal of all such unions is the realizing in the material realm of the dictum "all worlds, all times, all loves are one." In MacEwen's poetry praise is reserved for events and circumstances in which paradoxes such as that of the beast poem above are maintained—for circumstances in which, for example, the divine and the mortal are one, man and woman are one, or process and stasis are one. The latter paradox is particularly common.

> in that sublayer of sense
> where there is no time
> no differentiation of identities
> but co-presents, a static recurrence
> (that wolf is stone, this
> stone is wolf) (*BB*, 31)

This is the paradox she used to praise her fellow poet Al Purdy in "The Winemaker"; he moves but he is also static, "always returning."

> the winemaker comes to Toronto
>   disguised as a dervish to chase himself
> back and forth across the urgent purple city, a living query
> of his own movement—like those poems of his that go

> round and round and where they stop nobody
> guesses—
> ....
> (there is the man. he returns,
> he is always returning) (*BB*, 38)

The "returning" paradox allows Purdy here to approach the dervish, the dancing Siva; earlier in the poem it let him assume the role of Frazer's Maimed King, "With one foot on the pavement/and the other poised for flight" (*BB*, 38) and thus contain briefly another paradox, the divine in the mortal.

"Turning" itself is a frequent term in MacEwen's poems, and invariably is used to present the same paradoxical image as the "returning" above. We are dreamers "in the turning wilderness of time," she writes in "Dreamer Dream On" (*SM*, 51). She is even more explicit about the meaning of "turning" in "Dream Three: the Child," where she asks a figure outside her window,

> ...why are you turning and turning and turning
> getting nowhere fast on that wheel
> When you could be talking to me?
>
> I've always been here, turning and turning
> and I'll always be here, turning and turning
> From the beginning and to the end turning,
> from alpha to omega turning and turning.
> and I looked and I saw it was me. (*SM*, 56)

The Alpha to Omega reference binds the poem and the turning image to other totality-enclosing paradoxes in "Noman" (*N*, 88-89) and in the epigraph to *Julian the Magician.*

So frequently are the union of opposites, the duality of truth, the inverse way to knowledge, and the wisdom of paradox mentioned in MacEwen's poetry that they unquestionably become its major themes. But their mere presence as ideas within the poetry does not in any way ensure the success of the poetry. To declare the value of the unspeakable is not the same as to speak the unspeakable. The power of MacEwen's fiction rested not in the halting attempts of its characters to announce arcane truth, but in the convincing vividness with which she made these characters seem to be living lives of mythic preoccupation. The unspeakable myths were "spoken" by MacEwen by making them live in the pages of those novels and stories. There in the drama and concrete settings of her art the mythic penetrated, took residence in, the actual.

It is this sense of drama and actuality which is sometimes missing from MacEwen's poetry. The paradoxes and theories of opposites often appear merely as theorems, possibly believed in by their writer, but without flesh, feeling, or life.

> when touch is merest wish we swim
> like fish, our seed the liquid night
> the length of seas, our first deep element
> and love is the end of sleep and sight (*SM*, 71)

Sometimes there is emotion evident, but without any apparent motivation or context, as in this passage entitled "Tesla, an Excerpt from a Verse Play."

> I see the whole universe
> As a series of alternating currents—
> Negative and positive poles volleying
> for power, supplementing each other
> —their terrific arguments—
> Negative and positive poles
> —their splended dialectic—
> Magnetic fields dragging their planets
> around them (*BB*, 19)

The title, of course, partially excuses this passage's circumstantial vagueness, but there are many other poems not so titled which also read like mysteriously excerpted dialogue from a hidden play.

all orbits complement
the logic we derive
from eggshell symmetry
of satellite or sweet
concentric circles
of crumbs and insects
on cosmic tablecloths;

begins "Nikolayev and Popovich" (*RF,* 11). Maybe "all orbits" do, but the point remains dogma much as Akhenaton's "the force within the Aton is both contained and uncontained" (*KEKD,* 41) remains dogma. And the condition of believing dogma, which is fully rendered in the novel, and which alone could have given power to the poem, is not evident, and apparently not wanted.

This is the greatest flaw of MacEwen's first two books, *Selah* (1961) and *The Drunken Clock* (1961), and a persistent vice in her third, *The Rising Fire.* Flights of emotion and dogmatic statements of belief are offered without hint of what may have brought them into being. The music of the language and the force of the imagery are supposed to move one to insights which in the poet were circumstantially created. They do not.

All the fine young horses
crumble when the clocks leap
and clocks will not sleep
to let them pass, manes fumbled
in wind and birthday. (*RF,* 17)

But also in these early books are a number of concrete experiential poems—"The Death Agony of the Butterfly," "Two Horses," "Beach" —which show that MacEwen was aware of the power of the lyric poem to convey drama as well as deliver statement. These poems foreshadow a large number of poems in *A Breakfast for Barbarians* which have such a detailed dramatic quality that any mythic content is given to the reader as experience and in no way as simple description of opinion or of emotional condition.

It is later poems like these, which present myth as the poet's own literal experience, as something she has lived as vividly and as credibly as did Julian or Akhenaton, which form the essential part of her poetic work. In many of these poems the dramatic element is underlined by the poet's placing herself in the poem as a character among other characters, as in "The Left Hand and Hiroshima."

> Asked once why I fanned my fingers before my eyes
> to screen the strange scream of them, I, sinister, replied,
> Recently I dropped a bomb on Hiroshima. (*BB*, 26)

Most of these poems, like the above, begin in a realistic circumstance. "Wombs" begins "She had this little red bean with 10 ivory animals in it/carved in India" (*BB*, 8). "The Astronauts" begins "Now his orbit exceeds three" (*BB*, 17). Most also are built on casual, if not homey, detail throughout their length. So constructed are "Appendectomy" (*BB*, 42), "The Peanut Butter Sandwich" (*BB*, 34), and even the exuberant and apocalyptic "A Breakfast for Barbarians":

> to gaze at each other over the rust-heap of cutlery,
> drinking a coffee that takes an eternity—
> till, bursting, bleary,
> we laugh, barbarians, and rock the universe—
> and exclaim to each other over the table
> over the table of bones and scrap metal
> over the gigantic junk-heaped table:
>
> by God that was a meal (*BB*, 1)

Finally, all of these are written in a relaxed, colloquial, witty, and occasionally racy language that seems suited to the drama of the circumstances. Gone is the inflated poetic language of the first two books which presented MacEwen as a variation on the ecstatic dryad, and in its place impressively realistic speech which presents her as a most attractive flesh and blood woman.

alas, we have too many myths
    and we know that too. but it is breakfast.
I am with you. care for another? (*BB*, 34)

In such poems the miracle of the transubstantiation is achieved; the mythic is made flesh. MacEwen gives the myths substance by realizing on the page not them but herself who lives them. As readers we come to see the myths as kinetic (which is the only condition they can have if they are not to be dead and artifactual), as alive in the believably rendered experiences of the poet.

The Shadow Maker is a less successful book than *A Breakfast for Barbarians*. Few of the poems rise far above being essays about belief and feeling. None have the passion and energy of the best of the previous book. There are a number, however, that do possess the power of actual experience—"Invocations," "The Name of the Place," "The Compass," "Night on Gull Lake," and particularly "Dream One: the Man-Fish" and "Dream Two: the Beasts."

The most revealing characteristic of MacEwen's most recent book of poetry, *Armies of the Moon*, is that it is nearly impossible to excerpt any abstract statement of belief from it. She has turned here almost entirely to dramatic and indirect means. The themes of the book are similar to those given abstract expression earlier, but here they are for the most part presented in action. The Siva-like dance into secret knowledge is embodied in a highly visual and colloquial account of a Toronto nightclub performer:

the very gay *kallitechnis*, which is to say
performer
in the Greek nightclub
has the last laugh, tho' we're in *fits*
when he does a little belly dance across the stage
....
nobody gets right into Laki's eyes
where some primeval knowledge lingers, old
hermaphroditic dreams and Oh so lively sins
of Sodom and Athens and East Toronto (*AM*, 16-17)

The paradoxical love-death, creation-destruction concept is contained in a number of "domestic detail" poems reminiscent of the very strongest poems of *A Breakfast for Barbarians*. In the key poem of this cluster, "Phobos," MacEwen begins,

> Last week lightning clove the mighty tree
> outside my house, and the leaves turned in
> surrendering their white sides; I learned
> that lightning cleaves what it most loves
> and cuts in half what it means to caress (*AM*, 24)

This idea is repeated in "Dining at the Savarin," where MacEwen finds herself consuming her forebears, devouring "the guts and claws of creatures which preceded me":

> . . . I'm amazed
> with what venom I crack open the corpse of this white crab
> the sound like a bark of protest from some prehuman world
> and how loudly I suck the sweet meat from the hollow
> of its claw. (*AM*, 12)

It is also in "Sea Things" where, preparing to eat a can of oysters, "naked and embryonic," she comments

> . . . they flung me forth, a nuisance in their midst
> with my mind and complex hungers
> crashing on the high white beaches of the world. (*AM*, 11)

It recurs in a modified form in "The Vacuum Cleaner Dream" in which the poet sees herself "vacuuming the universe" and finding later in the bag of the machine "the sleeping body of my love" (*AM*, 18).

Central to *Armies of the Moon* is the thesis that in hostility, violence, and warfare, man indulges the shadow side of his selfhood—his darkness, his lunar self—and fails to strive toward his bipolar potential. One of the weaker and essayistic poems of the book tells us

"The moon was a cup from which we drank/the silver milk of night" and associates the moon with martyrs, war, bullets, and the Roman lance which pierced Christ's side (*AM*, 29). Two much stronger poems present this idea concretely. One, "The Film," points to the "silver screen" of the movie theatre as the lunar face of man's violent dreams, a screen duplicated in the "dark theatres" of human blood. "The silver reel unravels in your skull,"

> your flesh becomes a screen
> the drama unfolds
> along your fingers
> and across your open palm the armies run
> and down your veins the false blood falls;
> I want to tell you—
> this is the kind of war nobody needs. (*AM*, 42)

A second poem, "The Other Underground," shows MacEwen ruthlessly exposing the dark or lunar side of her own self, the side which justified her statement in *A Breakfast for Barbarians*, "I dropped a bomb upon Hiroshima." This poem employs explicit dream-waking, dark-light, moon-sun, silver-gold imagery to make clear that in waging war man indulges his other, his shadow, at the expense of the authentic light.

> who will absolve me of the crimes
> which I commit each night in dreams?
> not you, my dark associates
> who shade your eyes with many flags
> and do not see these nests of lightning
> in the trees.

Man's collective evil lurks within the dreams and soul even of the poet.

> tell me what the dark committees of my soul are plotting
> and where the guerillas of my guilt are hiding out—
> for I remember that the cockpit of the plane
> was silent in Hiroshima,
> as silent as my skull...

The evil performs a reverse alchemy, transforming intelligence into brutality, light into darkness, sunlight into lunar shadow. At Hiroshima,

> . . . the man sitting in the sun somewhere
> *dissolved* and left the black atomic shadow
> of his soul upon the stairs.

By the end of the poem such testimony, plus that of other lunar images—"the midnights lit by warlight, scarlet stars/the sheer hallucination of our wars"—fully supports MacEwen's declaration ". . . the Enemy is where he always was—/in the black lunar landscape of our mirrors" (*AM*, 34-35).

Several of the later poems in the book reintroduce alchemy's divine Mercurius, but with a clearer relevancy than elsewhere in her poetry. For the obvious remedy for a world fully sickened by black or lunar light, by the lunacy of surreal destruction, is the introduction of a reconciling light which will subsume rather than oppose the darkness. Thus in "Jewellery" MacEwen announces "I want/to be the prisoner of gold" (*AM*, 53); and in "House of Mercury" she asks that "all those who come to me/ should wear the blue of metal or the quick/silver of the sea which gluts its mineral histories," that is, that they should seek to recreate in themselves the mercurial ("quick silver") fountain, the *aqua permanens*, out of which the Mercurius is traditionally born. As the sea breaks down and combines the metals that fall into it, so she would become water in order to transmute the silver moon and her earthly weaponry to the quicksilver source of the healing god.

> Leave me be, I want to be water,
> I'm trying to flow though I'm dense and silver,
> I'm trying to move a ton of metal
> as easily as the sea. (*AM*, 52)

Five poems later, in a work reminiscent of the story "The Oarsman and the Seamstress," a sleeping man whom she watches attains a union of passion and art, of war and prophecy, of divinity and mortality, resembling that of the alchemical lord.

> He lies there accomplished and unknown,
> his limbs arranged by passion and by art,
> a fluid beauty he inhabits all alone.
> The dark bird of war is dormant in his loins
> and prophets reside in the seeds of his kiss;
>   the generations of his mouth are legion
>   yet his body is inviolably his. (*AM*, 57)

Armies of the Moon concludes with a nine-poem verse play that was begun in *A Breakfast for Barbarians*, "The Nine Arcana of the Kings." The speakers are an Egyptian prince and his sister to whom he is married; these may be Smenkhare and Meritaton of *King of Egypt, King of Dreams* although it must be said that a very few of the details of the poem contradict such an interpretation.[2] Millenia after the prince's murder and his internment by his wife, her faithful vigil for him in "the house beside the river" (a summer house in Meru Alton?) is rewarded by his return "undead, unborn." The prince appears now to be another Mercurius, combining divinity and substantiality, the "awful sun" associated with his father (logically Akhenaton) with the "moon" associated with his sister. However, he may also be, like Julian, an unhappy Mercurius, for his wife says that he now wears

> . . . the cursed crown
> ....
> the double crown of those who wear
> the kingdoms of heaven and hell on their head (*AM*, 64-72)

We are reminded of *The Shadow Maker's* opening epigraph, taken from Carl Jung, one that can apply equally to Julian or to this prince: "It is 'a fearful thing to fall into the hands of the living God.'"

The indirect and dramatic artistry of "The Nine Arcana of the Kings" and of many other poems in *Armies of the Moon* suggests that MacEwen may be getting much closer to "speaking the unspeakable" than her Akhenaton ever did. The artistic problem here centres in the fact that when one speaks the unspeakable as idea or formula, as does Akhenaton to his disciples, it is not communicated—and therefore is in a very real sense not spoken. But when one uses speech to imaginatively convey an action in which the unspeakable is imminent, then it is communicated without being literally spoken. This is why Christ taught in parables, and why the plays of Shakespeare have shaped more lives than the essays of Bacon. The problem, as MacEwen should have known from her occult studies very early in her career, is to make the word incarnate. Just as Christ must seek the living body of Julian to realize his myth, so MacEwen has had to seek the flesh of situation to give the ideas of her poetry living artistic form. I had never cared for her poetry until the vigorous actuality of *A Breakfast for Barbarians*, and later thought *The Shadow Maker* contained more shadow than art. But *King of Egypt, King of Dreams, Noman,* and *The Armies of the Moon* demonstrate that presently the alchemical secret and the secret of art—that the god must reside equally in the phenomenal and the numinal worlds—is in her possession. I look forward to her using this secret again.

---

1. The narrative point of view is the most unsatisfactory aspect of the novel. In the opening pages the narrator relates from Julian's viewpoint, then rapidly shifts to knowing the motives and feelings of all the characters equally. Late in the novel the narrator knows so little of what Julian is thinking or experiencing that Julian's diary has to be appended. Perhaps we are to believe that Julian's mind becomes increasingly inaccessible to the unnamed narrator as Christ's usurpation of Julian's consciousness proceeds. However, such a conjecture neither is encouraged by the author nor excuses the inconsistency of the point of view early in the novel.

2. The most troublesome detail is the prince's statement that he killed his father. Otherwise, the sun associations of his father, the father's being called "our mad forgotten father," the prince's marriage to his sister, his murder in a temple "between the fountain and the pillars," his burial by his wife, the jackal seals on his tomb, the necklaces the princess associates with their love-making, and the bed of "ebony and straw" on which they make love are all consistent with the portrait of Smenkhare and her Meritaton in the novel.

IMPRESSIONABLE REALISM: THE STORIES OF CLARK BLAISE

When I first attempted a commentary on Clark Blaise's stories, I was, like most of his reviewers, drawn immediately to summarize the themes and issues these stories raise. A United States view of Canada. A continental sensibility. A search for place. A North American education. Blaise invites such an approach through the titles of his books which propose not character (as in Munro's *Lives of Girls and Women*) or place (as in Hood's *Around the Mountain*) but abstract concept—justice, education —as the primary underlying element of the works. In *Tribal Justice* the reader is directed to look for the 'justice' —both real and ironic—meted out to their members and non-members by contemporary North American kinship groups; in *A North American Education* he is directed to look at a process of cultural conditioning and to discern what is specifically 'North American' about the values being conditioned.

Both titles turn attention away from the stories as *écriture* and away from the author as writer. In this they reflect a general effort in

Blaise's writing to render invisible the linguistic surface of the writing, its narrative structure, and its fictional strategies. In most of the stories a narrator comes between the reader and the writer—the rhythms, the diction, the syntax, the narrative direction and sequence all become ostensibly those of this narrator. In most, the language has a relaxed, non-literary tone, one we associate with the anecdotal newspaper column or private journal rather than the short story. In most, there is no central incident around which the story has been formed and in which its meaning has been concentrated; a Blaise story often ends without the traditional 'climax' and gains power from this lack. In none of Blaise's stories are there any overt uses of symbolism, metaphor, or non-factual imagery.

At their beginnings, many of Blaise's creations do not appear to be serious short stories. Blaise achieves this masking of intent by genre blending. The story will begin as if it were a reflective essay, and contain little hint of plot or situation for the first half-page or page. There will be a voice, reflecting, considering—more informal than Montaigne's but sharing his intensity and unpredictability.

> In a certain season (the late winter) and in certain areas (those fringes between the city core and the river that makes it an island) Montreal is the ugliest city in the world. Despite its reputation, its tourist bureaus, most of the island of Montreal will break your heart. Most of us live with broken hearts, thumping little fists constricting our throats. In this, Montreal is truly the Paris of North America. The same bleakness, the same *bidonvilles* stretching for miles beyond the city walls. Our dreams had always been salvation and *bonheur*, even knowing that we'd ingested the worst of both worlds: the suspicions and ignorance of the *petit commerçant*, with the arrogant spawl of America.
>
> ("Among the Dead," *TJ*, 219)

Other Blaise stories indicate plot from the beginning but have the tone not of the literary story but of anecdotal journalism.

> There are families on the lake who've blasted crannies into the soaring granite cliffs a hundred feet above the water: Germans who thread their way like mountain goats balancing a weekend's beer on their heads, who dive like Acapulco professionals from a board on their porch into the unsounded depths below. I have watched them in summers past from the wide porch of our cabin on the low marshy shore across the way—fat men of fifty in bikini briefs walking to the board, their laughter and joking clear, if foreign, from a mile away.
>
> ("At the Lake," *TJ*, 200)

The distinction between Blaise's writing and such journalism lies in the seriousness of the engagement. Both Blaise and the journalist adopt a disarming tone: the narrative will be amusing, puzzling perhaps, but not disconcerting.

> ...I envied Serge, who hadn't missed a weekend at the cabin in fifteen years. Every weekend he added cubits to his lands, his sewage, his dockery, his cabin, his soul, whereas I—a younger man more aware a thousand times of ravages, impurity, and decay—have found the battle, or challenge, overwhelming. I had to ask myself what did I really want: electric blankets, pavement, stove and fridge? And I say no, of course not; I wanted my son to grow up with nature. Skier, swimmer, fisherman, even hunter; I wanted him to grow up unflawed. I wanted the lake accessible yet remote, I wanted my cabin rustic but livable, I wanted a granite resolve to do on my marshy store what the Germans had done on their cliffs; yet I wanted never to lose my immemorial torpor, my hours of dozing on a creaky dock peering at carp through the widening cracks.
>
> (*TJ*, 200-201)

For the journalist, however, to be disarming is his final intent; for Blaise, it is a deceit that prepares for inevitable disruptions— disruptions that will be especially devastating because of their contrast to the illusory innocence of the world they have entered. Vandals invade the summer cabin. In the spring the narrator returns to clean and repair it. The hints about his self-observed weakness increase. "I wanted to call out to Erika, as though she were with me—as though I had confided all my fears—'It's safe. We made it through another winter.'" (*TJ*, 207)

The blending of subliterary or nonliterary genres with the short story form is particularly noticeable in those Blaise stories narrated in the first person—a viewpoint which increasingly appears to be the dominant one in Blaise's work. Three of the ten stories in *A North American Education* are told from a third-person viewpoint, one from the second person (which, because it addresses the reader directly, has the effect of a first-person narration), and the remaining six from the first person. In his second book, *Tribal Justice*, all but one of the twelve stories is related from the first person. The nonliterary effect is especially possible in the first-person narration because, at the story's opening, the reader is invited inside not by a professional writer, but one of the characters. This is a subtle distinction, but an important one for the fiction of innocent technique which Blaise practises. The reader is beckoned to from within the story, rather than directed into it from the outside. His relationship to the narrator is intimate, the narrator is fully active in the story, his personality and limitations are revealed in it. Most important, the narrator reveals himself as a nonliterary person whose interest is in retelling the story rather than in making it, who, because of his personal stake in the action, is engaged more by what happened than by any search for impressive means of presentation.

The narrator in a Blaise story is an innocent. He seems incapable of, sometimes incapacitated for, literary deceit. His sentences meander, almost outside of his own control.

> I am moved by that in art, in life; by the slow revelation of a larger design, the way we live one detail at a time and never know the depth and the extent—the meaning—of what we have made. Every life a universe unrevealed, as well as a simple, repetitive design. I am more patient with design than I was ten years ago.
>
> ("The March," *TJ*, 121)

His narratives lack direction, economy; they bog down in reflection and analysis; they circle and evade the events to which a professional narrator might want his reader to attend. Essentially, a Blaise narrator is not interested in telling the story; he is interested in analyzing it, savouring it, reflecting on it. This aspect gives the story two concurrent levels of plot—one that involves the events being recounted and another in which the recounting itself is the central event.

A Blaise narrator is a man who, in "Words for the Winter," lives "in dreams," whose grip on this world is tentative and painful, much like his grip on the sentence or on the narrative line.

> Something infinitely small but infinitely complicated has happened to our lives, and I don't know how to present it— in its smallness, in its complication—without breaking down. I who live in dreams have suffered something real, and reality hurts like nothing in this world.
>
> (*NAE*, 37)

His control over factual reality is dubious and limited—he is usually dissatisfied with his dress, his home furnishings, his body, his ability as a father. He feels committed only "to trivia" (*NAE*, 47). In the case where the narrator reveals himself to be a professional writer, his anxieties about his writing and his sense of its aimlessness reinforce the reader's sense of the spontaneity and guilelessness of his narration. This is Paul Keeler again:

> I used to write miniature novels, vividly imagined, set anywhere my imagination moved me. Then something slipped. I started writing only of myself and these vivid moments in a confusing flux.
>
> ("Going to India," *NAE*, 73)

The child version of this narrator possesses, in addition to the child's normal awe of the adult world, the same doubts about his ability to find self-confidence and respect. The environment of this boy offers neither acceptable models of self-confident masculinity nor opportunity for him to experience for himself confidence-building successes. His father in all of the stories is weak, unperceptive, unrealistic, and unsuccessful. He allows himself to be swindled by moneylenders, misled by promoters. He pursues success both arrogantly and lethargically, trusting that it can be acquired by the most minimal of efforts. "He greedily sought the sun, grew brown and striking, and felt that he had planted himself in fortune's path and had only to stay put and success would stumble across him" ("The Fabulous Eddie Brewster," *TJ*, 34). The successful male characters, like Eddie Brewster himself, are corrupt and unscrupulous. The boy's personal and independent attempts to develop self-confidence are undermined by his father's wanderings from job to job and his tearing of the boy from every new environment before he can gain the knowledge to deal with it. The boy begins to masochistically love his own smallness, and to seek out activities and situations which will humiliate and diminish him. Here is the young Norman Dyer of "Grids and Doglegs":

> Astronomy is the moral heavyweight of the physical sciences; it is a humiliating science, a destroyer of pride in human achievements, or shame in human failings. Compared to the vacant dimensions of space—of time, distance, and temperature—what could be felt for Eisenhower's heart attack, Grecian urns, 6 million Jews, my waddle and shiny gabardines. My parents were nearing separation, their store beginning to falter—what could I care for their silence, their fights, the begging for bigger and bigger loans?
>
> (*TJ*, 49-51)

Paradoxically, the activity he chooses here for self-abasement, and which he believes to dwarf his personal humiliations, continues to lead back to them. The syntax moves him inevitably to his own "waddle and shiny gabardines." His diction moves him from the vacancies of space to the silences of his parents' marriage. His belief that his love of intellectual and abstract humiliation is greater and more noble than his everyday wounds is thus played off against the reader's growing knowledge that these wounds inform the entirety of Norman's attachments to such humiliation.

In Blaise's first-person narratives every element contributes to the characterization of the narrator. The narrator defines himself in the words he chooses, the sentences he develops. Style becomes character. In "He Raises Me Up" the style reveals a man who maintains some minimal equanimity through irony, and who, when physical reality has betrayed him, rushes gladly into the sureties of parallel phrases and rhetorical syntax.

> Cars are an apt measurement of the inner man. Blessed are the carless. Like dwellers in high-rises, their every need at hand, never required to answer an unmonitored door, to touch a shovel, to call a heating company. Never to mow, to paint, to polish, never to fret over plumbing and roof. Radiantly helpless. Fortunate too are the tinkerers, grown men driving around with tool chests in their trunks, those grease-stained knuckles, those teen-age tatoos under the business suits. Rapturously self-reliant. And for the rest of us there comes a moment when we prowl the vacant city in a cashmere coat, doubling back over a deserted bridge where any witness would take you for a potential suicide. Flagging at cars that spray your shoes with a gray pasty slime. *Clown*, you tell yourself.
>
> (*TJ*, 210)

The narrative structure of the story also becomes characterization. "He Raises Me Up" has an erratic narrative line, opening with three basically factual paragraphs in reverse chronology about an automobile breakdown, followed by one paragraph of philosophical discourse and fantasy, two of distant memory, another which returns to the 'present' of the first three paragraphs, then a series of paragraphs about a recalled visit to a dentist, another philosophical reflection, a return to the present of the stranded automobile, and so on. The narrator lives in fantasy and memory as much as in the present. He appears to exist in the present only when distracted by the sounds of voices or the motions of objects away from his reveries and reflections. The story does not have a climax. After the narrator concludes what are to him humiliating negotiations with the tow-truck driver, the passive car is towed away, its temporally disoriented driver and his wife sprawled within. "How peaceful is this surrender, stretched out on the front seat, feet up, head against the cool moist window, holding Erika in both arms, swaying in the metal sling of my broken car." The lack of climax becomes another way of characterization. Nothing can be climactic to one whose hold on the present is so tenuous. For this man, the present is not substantial enough to form itself into pattern and climax.

This method of characterization and kind of narrator is the usual one in Blaise's fiction. The narrator is passive, reflective, non-dogmatic—an observer rather than a controller of events. He is often a young boy puzzled by the scale and values of the adult world ("The Bridge," "A Salesman's Son Grows Older"), or a young man who feels vaguely alien from his peers and uncomfortable about social rituals ("Grids and Doglegs," "The March"). When he is a thirty-year-old adult, he is still possessed of very 'young' feelings—passivity, weakness, inferiority. He feels overwhelmed by such tasks as home decorating, the improvement of a summer cabin, the repair of an automobile. He can feel smaller in the presence of a tow-truck driver, a political agitator, an adolescent girl who steals and mutilates his mail, an airline captain, or an outdoorsman who hangs guns and trophies on his wall.

In Blaise's third-person narratives this textual method of characterization is not present; he makes no attempt in these to use the conventions of consistent interior monologue which could bring such characterization into being. In "The Seizure" the narration begins in the first person, but this narrator vanishes after a page and before he can be at all known to the reader. An undefined omniscient narrator takes over, who on most occasions writes from outside the characters, but on other occasions can enter into the perspectives of three of the major characters. The invisibility of the narrator in this story disconnects his words and emphases from any personal, motivational context and creates for the reader a sense of arbitrariness which he does not encounter in the first-person viewpoint. The character portrayals which the voice of the story consciously offers seem no more or less trustworthy than elsewhere but, unlike in the first-person story, these characterizations cannot be understood by the reader as part of one greater characterization whose trustworthiness is based on self-betrayal in the medium of the text. Such greater characterizations, whatever the point of view, are assigned by a narrator and remain relative to this narrator's perceptual ability.

In "A Class of New Canadians," although the anonymous narrator writes only from the perspective of the central character, he emphasizes his distance from this character by repeating his surname, Dyer, in every context in which the reader expects 'he.' Again, because of the anonymity of the narrator and his distinctness from the point-of-view character, the potential of the syntax, style, and structure to be aspects of characterization remains unexplored. In "A Continent of Strangers" the possibility that the third-person narrator is the main character disguised by the conventions of interior monologue is repeatedly broken by the introduction of information which this character, Paul Keeler, cannot credibly possess. For example, Keeler is a newcomer to Europe, but the narrative voice is able to tell us, "Place Pigalle—one place where an American can encounter France—was still dusty at 7:30, not jammed, not festive" (*NEA*, 103). The reader is thus reminded that the actual narrator is anonymous, has no personal involvement in the action of the story, and that the technical surface of the writing is in no way related to the characterizing language of the story's central participant.

Because of his avoidance of metaphor, simile, and romantic imagery, Clark Blaise always presents a physically precise and vivid perspective. The intensity of this vividness, however, is greater in the first-person narratives than in the third-person ones, and often appears to depend on the innocence of neutrality of this first-person narrator. Feeling alienated from the physical world, and often intimidated by it, this narrator observes with the care and fascination of a traveller in hostile lands; the smallest detail may save him from embarrassment or disaster.

> We sped to his cabin and had a beer. There were two large rooms, one for cooking and eating with floor to ceiling windows looking out on the lake, and an elevated unwindowed room with a high-beamed ceiling containing a wood-burning fireplace, bunk beds covered with animal skins, a guncase, and some mounted trophies. On the dining table I saw a freshly cut loaf of the round white bread they sell by the roadsides up north, a pot of still warm coffee, and Henri Troyat's *Tolstoi* in Livre de Poche.
>
> ("At the Lake," *TJ*, 202)

Because of the narrator's weak sense of selfhood, these masses of detail are innocently perceived; that is, they are contaminated by little connotative attribution or by any hint of pathetic fallacy. The narrator projects nothing of himself into them; he yields to them, allows them to pass through him. Being only themselves, these details come to the reader in the same weight and sharpness of outline with which they assault the narrator. The result is both an underlining of the ineffectuality of narrator as a character and an extraordinarily luminous presentation of phenomena.

> The women have gathered around the body; little pieces are offered to them from the head and entrails. The pigs' heads are pink, perhaps they've been boiled, and hairless. The eyes are strangely blue. You remove your gloves and touch the skin, you brush against the grainy ear. How the eye attracts you! How you would like to lift one out, press its smoothness against your tongue, then crush it in your mouth. And you cannot. Already your finger is numb and the head, it seems, has shifted under you. And the eye, in panic, grows white as your finger approaches.
>
> ("Eyes," *NAE*, 23-23)

The necessary basis for a thematic interpretation of Blaise's stories lies in this innocent narrator, in the meanderings of his narratives, and in his impressionable realism. Readers who see in Blaise's stories a parable about the North American condition —about rootlessness, homelessness, about dislocating contrasts to be found among juxtaposing groups within North American culture—are generalizing the particular lives of his narrators into metaphor. This generalizing is invited by Blaise not only in his titles but also in the various epigraphs he includes in *A North American Education*, as in the following from Pascal.

> 'We do not rest satisfied with the present. We anticipate the future as too slow in coming, as if in order to hasten its course; or we recall the past, to stop its too rapid flight. So imprudent are we that we wander in the times which are not ours, and do not think of the only one which belongs to us; and so idle are we that we dream of those times which are no more, and thoughtlessly overlook that which alone exists.'
>
> (*NAE*, 39)

The peculiar multi-cultural ambience of Blaise's stories is based mostly on his successful attribution to his narrators of an insecure sense of self. The narrator who feels alien in Florida, Cincinnati, Saskatchewan, Montreal, Quebec City, Germany, Sweden, or India is before all else the boy who feels small beside his baseball-playing fellow students or the man who feels weak beside a Peugeot dealer with mysterious skills.

> As we talk he cuts little wedges of pine to shore up our cabin and make the door fit tighter. He cuts cardboard to make the pump airtight. Unobtrusive skills I'll never master. Lurid stories I can only hope to copy, of gamblers in Acapulco, jail terms, a bankruptcy, an oath in an oxygen tent to be reborn.
>
> ("Words for the Winter," *NAE*, 26)

He is a man who at times feels alienated from his own body.

> A nerve ripped from my body at thirty. I am a young man, haven't deteriorated much since twenty-one, except to remain the same at least till thirty-five. But somehow, some day, some *minute*, the next long decline begins to set in. At forty I will be middle-aged. At forty-five, twenty-five years from my grave. When does it start—with a chipped tooth? A broken nose? A broken leg even? Oh, no. It begins in choices. The road downhill is slick with fat and fallen hair and little pills. Bad styles and bad convictions. Pain killers, contraceptives, tranquilizers, and weak erections. Pulled nerves.
>
> ("Extractions and Contractions," *NAE*, 45)

His personal insecurities in the face of a conventionally masculine world of baseball-hurling negroes, sexually aggressive strippers, Florida policemen, fishermen, hunters, and truck drivers are repeated in different disguises in the insecurities of a young writer among non-writers ("Continent of Strangers"), of a young professor among aggressive adult students ("A Class of New Canadians"), of an Americanized French-Canadian among militant Quebec nationalists ("The March") or of a university boy with sophisticated liberal views caught between a reactionary father and cynically Marxist negro truck driver ("The Seizure"). The effect of these associations is to create two contrasting clusters of images—one linking personal insecurity with art, education, cultural tolerance, sensitivity, and liberal politics, and the other linking aggressive masculinity with materialism, cultural chauvinism, insensitivity, and committed politics. Within these clusters, the personal insecurities and conflicts of the narrators become metaphors for the cultural insecurities and conflicts to which the titles of Blaise's collections allude. Curiously, stories which are notable for their lack of metaphor become, as units, metaphors for continental issues.

In terms of Blaise's stories, the gap between these two image clusters is unreconcilable; his narrators can at best, as in "Among the Dead," drive cautiously among the aggressive and philistine snow-removal trucks and accept, like Norman Dyer in "Words for the Winter," the fact that 'reality hurts.' The conclusion of the one story in which a narrator attempts a reconciliation can be viewed only as ironic. This is "The March," in which Pierre Desjardins, a displaced and Americanized French Canadian, mildly liberal, and sexually anxious, decides to give up all hope of reclaiming his Quebec heritage and to marry a young Bostonian civil-rights worker—a dogmatic, impulsive, and shallow girl. "It's crazy, isn't it," she says to him perceptively as he leads her back through the streets of Washington, D.C., to a civil-rights march bus, carries her up the steps, and thereby embraces the conventions of American politics, show-business, and marriage.

There is no doubt that characterization is the most important element in a Blaise story and its central intent. But it is not the static kind of characterization introduced to the short story earlier in the century by Joyce and Mansfield. It is not character revealed with photographic clarity in the betraying incident or epiphany. It is characterization as a condition of being. It is characterization revealed in the process of language, narrative sequence, choice of diction, choice of actions. Characterization in Blaise's best stories becomes style, syntax, diction, and structure; language and literary form become environments within which his narrators reveal both themselves and their visions of their cultures.

ATWOOD'S GORGON TOUCH

In the opening poem of Margaret Atwood's first book, *Double Persephone*, a "girl wih the gorgon touch" walks through a formal garden searching for "a living wrist and arm." But she finds only "a line of statues" with "marble flesh." This "gorgon" is apparently Medusa, whose glance turned men to stone. In the concluding poem of Atwood's recent collection of new work, *You Are Happy*, another male figure appears with similarly sculptural qualities:

> On the floor your body curves
> like that: the ancient pose, neck slackened, arms
> thrown above the head, vital
> throat and belly lying
> undefended. light slides over you,...

But this statue comes to life, is willed by the voice of the poem out of the worlds of art and ritual and into that of flesh.

this is not an altar, they are not
acting or watching

You are intact, you turn
towards me, your eyes opening, the eyes
intricate and easily bruised
("Book of Ancestors," 96)

In the seven books of poems which lie between these passages, this opposition between the static, the mythological, or the sculptural and the kinetic, the actual, or the temporal has been a central concern. Atwood's consideration of this opposition has been simultaneously ethical and aesthetic; all attitudes toward form in her work have been subject to moral judgements. The sources of this antithesis lie in the earliest days of Anglo-American modernism. Its deepest roots are in T. E. Hulme's rejection of nineteenth-century empathetic realism for "some geometrical shape which lifts him (man) out of the transience of the organic" and in the searches of Proust for "the real without being of the present moment" and of Pound for "a fragment of time in its pure state." Throughout Margaret Atwood's poetry such goals are presented as attractive, attainable—in terms of both life and poetic form—but ultimately unsatisfying. The formal garden can be created and entered but its marble flesh cannot be lifted from still dance into dancing life. Roles for lovers can be created and enacted in *Power Politics*, but the enactments cannot be relieved of a stylization which Atwood characterizes as both artistic and deadly. The lovers become lifeless statues.

Your face is silver
and flat, scaled like a fish

The death you bring me
is curved, it is the shape
of doorknobs, moons,
glass paperweights

> Inside it, snow and lethal
> flakes of gold fall endlessly
> over an ornamental scene
> a man and woman, hands joined and running.
> ("He is Last Seen," 56)

In "Progressive Insanities of a Pioneer" a farm can be created in formal images of fences and furrows, but it cannot be obliged to yield an ordered life. Here not only does art not bear life but it loses even its own sterile order and predictability when shattered by "the unnamed whale" of temporality and process.

This kind of poem, which makes up the bulk of Atwood's work, is overtly and normatively concerned with aesthetics— the role of the artist, the nature of form, and form's relationship to historical time. One can choose the aesthetics of space—style, sculpture, ritual, static beauty—or the aesthetics of time—flesh, earth, and process.

> Love, you must choose
> Between two immortalities:
> One of earth, lake, trees
> Feathers of a nameless bird
> The other of a world of glass,
> Hard marble, carven word. (*DP*, 131)

Many of Atwood's poems rest on this antithesis. "The animals in that country," "ceremonial," "elegant," "heraldic," "fixed in their tapestry of manners," are posed against the animals of "this country" that have "the faces of animals" and eyes that "flash once in car headlights/ and are gone" (*AC*, 2-3). In "At the Tourist Center in Boston," a "white relief map" of Canada "with red dots for the cities" is posed against a reality of "slush, / machines and assorted garbage" (*AC*, 18-19).

The imagery of alienation from process is even more overtly presented in "Totems" where the antithesis is between restored museum-display totempoles and an unrestored totempole fallen and neglected. The former are described as "static," "uprooted and transplanted" and as analogous to the tourists— "the other wooden people"—who pose nearby "for each others' cameras;" the latter is said to have "a / life in the progressing / of old wood back to / the earth, obliteration / that the clear-hewn / standing figures lacked." The images are again the sculptural—"clean-hewn," "static," "pose"—versus the temporal —"decay," "progressing." The poles have been taken out of time (uprooted both from the earth and from the culture which created them) and inserted into space—into a "park," into "cameras," and into "replicas and souvenirs" ("Some Objects of Wood and Stone," *The Circle Game*, 59-60).

The camera, as above, is a frequent symbol in Atwood for the conversion of time into space. The poem "Camera" describes a "cameraman" who in his search for an "organized instant" asks all reality to "stop," "hold still."

> you ask me to stop walking
> and compose me on the lawn
>
> you insist
> that the clouds stop moving
> the wind stop swaying the church
> on its boggy foundations
> the sun hold still in the sky

His subject, however, insists in turn that the spatial correlative which the camera creates is itself a participant in temporality.

> Wherever you partly are
> now, look again
> at your souvenir,
> your glossy square of paper
> before it dissolves completely:

Despite the time-fixing and light-fixing act of photography, historical time moves at nearly "the speed of light" to ravage both the photograph and the objects the cameraman hoped to save from time; ultimately the church is reduced to "a pile of muddy rubble / in the foreground" and the woman to a "small black speck / travelling towards the horizon / at almost the speed of light" (*CG*, 45-46).

Two other poems that use photographs with disappearing subjects to argue the imcompatibility of the art-object with temporality are "This is a Photograph of Me" and "Girl and Horse, 1928." In the first the "drowned" narrator claims to be "in the lake, in the center of the picture, just under the surface" —presumably under the surfaces of both the lake and the photo. Her appearance in the photograph is not a spatial phenomenon; it takes place in time—"if you look long enough / eventually / you will be able to see me" (*CG*, 11). Temporality lurks, we may conclude, under the deceptively solid surfaces of appearance. In "Girl and Horse, 1928," the poem's voice speaks from outside the photo to its girl-subject, insisting that her smile and her peaceful surroundings are illusory.

> Why do you smile? Can't you
> see the apple blossoms falling around
> you, snow, sun, snow, listen, the tree
> dies and is being burnt...

Like the formal garden of *Double Persephone*, such illusion is an attractive one. In actuality the "instant" of the photo ceases immediately:

> (on the other side
> of the picture, the instant
> is over, the shadow
> of the tree has moved. You wave,
>
> then turn and ride
> out of sight through the vanished
> orchard,...

But its illusion of permanence can bewitch the human mind, can become a "secret / place where we live, where we believe / nothing can change, grow older." The girl rides from the orchard "still smiling," in apparently happy ignorance of time's effects (*Procedures for Underground*, 10).

As one reads through Margaret Atwood's body of poems, one finds her constructing a catalogue of evasions, evasions that are all extensions of this human need to "believe nothing can change." All represent an aesthetics of space and denial of time. One is classical mythology—the formal gardens of Medusa in *Double Persephone* and Circe in "Circe / Mud Poems" of *You Are Happy*. Another is popular mythology—the Superman figure of "They Eat Out" in *Power Politics*, the comic book heroes wearing "rubber suits" of "Comic Books vs. History" in *Procedures for Underground*, or the "starspangled cowboy" with "porcelain grin" of "Backdrop Addresses Cowboy" in *The Animals in That Country*. Closely related is popular art—formulaic, "endless," and "stale."

> You take my hand and
> I'm suddenly in a bad movie,
> it goes on and on and
> why am I fascinated
>
> We waltz in slow motion
> through an air stale with aphorisms
> we meet behind endless potted palms
> you climb through the wrong windows (*PP*, 3)

Technology provides various ways of evading time. The camera, the blueprint ("The City Planners," *CG*, 27), or the museum ("The Circle Game," *CG*, 41; "A Night in the Royal Ontario Museum," *AC*, 20-21). A part of all of these is the philosophic evasion of humanism, the evasion of Atwood's pioneer who asserts man's timeless centrality in a processual nature palpably without centres. This poem, "Progressive Insanities of a Pioneer," contains Atwood's most vigorous portrait of the humanist:

> He stood, a point
> on a sheet of green paper

> proclaiming himself the center
> with no walls, no borders
> anywhere; the sky no height
> above him, totally un-
> enclosed
> and shouted:
>
> Let me out!

The pioneer's sensibilities are spatially oriented through the poem; he is appalled by the absence of walls and borders. He constructs a house, fences, furrows, in stubborn resistance to the fact that "unstructured space is a deluge." He attempts to name the objects in his environment—to use language's abstracting power to lift them out of time and into the spatial categories of generic reasoning. However, "Things / refused to name themselves, refused / to let him name them." Ultimately, time triumphs over space. The "unnamed whale" of process, Atwood tells us, bursts through his fences, his fields, his clearings, and his subject-object categorizing mind (*AC*, 36-39). By implication, the aesthetics of space and the ethics of the humanist ordering of space are also discredited. The land here is metaphorically the raw material of any art—of love, husbandry, architecture, poetry; the farmer is the artist/lover of *Double Persephone* with his choice between "earth, lake, trees" and "a world of glass, hard marble, carven wood."

The Journals of Susanna Moodie narrate a similar struggle between time and space. This theme is signalled in the opening poem in which Mrs. Moodie laments "the moving water will not show me / my reflection." She sees her adversaries as the sun ("The Planters," 16-17), change ("The Wereman," 19), unpredictability ("First Neighbours," 14-15), and "fire"—both literal fire and the fire of seasonal process ("The Two Fires," 22-23). She attempts to defend herself through time-denying form.

> ...concentrate on
> form, geometry, the human
> architecture of the house, square

> closed doors, proved roofbeams,
> the logic of windows (22)

But the "white chaos" (23) of her environment continually insists itself upon her as the only reality. Whiteness and light, frequent images in Atwood for camera-defying cosmic energy, surround and absorb her. A photograph taken in her old age documents her temporality rather than arresting it.

> I orbit
> the apple trees
> white white spinning
> stars around me
>
> I am being
> eaten away by light
> ("Daguerreotype Taken in Old Age," 48)

Susanna Moodie's death removes her from all possibility of spatial illusion—from walls, manners, categorizations, and clichés "set up...at intervals" (55); it confronts her with raw process—here, as elsewhere in Atwood, metaphorically termed "underground." "Underground" for Mrs. Moodie is a "blizzard," a "whirlwind," a "holy fire" ("Resurrection," 58-59). It moves her in the last lines of the book to declare war on spatial structure and location:

> I am the old woman
> sitting across from you on the bus,
> ....
> out of her eyes come secret
> hatpins, destroying
> the walls, the ceiling
>
> Turn, look down:
> there is no city
> this is the center of a forest

your place is empty
("A Bus Along St. Clair: December," 61)

Such imagery of 'underground' is one of Atwood's most important devices throughout her poetry for asserting the dominance of time over space. Time and process are subversive; they lurk under the surfaces of lakes, of photographs, under the ostensibly solid veneers of field and street. Process is liquid; substantiality—the basis of sculptural form—is an illusion man invents with his camera-eyes. Mrs. Moodie calls Canada "a land I floated on / but could not touch to claim" (30). The pioneer declares,

The land is solid
and stamped,

watching his foot sink
down through stone
up to the knee. (*AC*, 38)

Appearances are thus duplicitous; the appearance of stasis conceals process, the appearance of order conceals chaos, the appearance of solidity conceals liquidity, the appearance of predictability presages surprise. The double condition of 'double' Persephone, desiring process but receiving stone, is reversed for many of Atwood's later protagonists. The doubleness of reality for them lies in the invisible underpinning of temporality in ostensibly spatial objects. This doubleness requires a "double voice," one with "manners" and one with "knowledge" ("The Double Voice," *JSM*, 42) and possession of "procedures for underground." Time-transcending devices—mythology, art, imagination, stylization—must be recognized as either weapons or crutches used by the weak in the face of mutability.

Many Atwood poems imply, like "Girl and Horse, 1928," that the need to deny temporality is understandably human; many others present a persona who gives herself with zestful ironic self-awareness to games, poses, mythologies, and sculptural perceptions.

> We sit at a clean table
> eating thoughts from clean plates
>
> and see, there is my heart
> germfree, and transparent as glass
>
> and there is my brain, pure
> as cold water in the china
> bowl of my skull
> ("A Meal," *CG*, 33)

The persona of *Power Politics* has this kind of ironic awareness of her addiction to the aesthetics of the "circle game." Her lover is another of the men of stone that Atwood's 'gorgon' personae seem inevitably to encounter.

> You stay closed, your skin
> is buttoned firmly around you,
> your mouth is a tin decoration,
> you are in the worst possible taste
>
> You are as fake as the marble trim
> around the fireplace,... (*PP*, 44)

His determined attempts to transcend time sometimes involve commercial mythology—"suspended above the city / in blue tights and a red cape / eyes flashing in unison"—and at other times political mythology:

> in a year there will be nothing left
> of you but a megaphone
>
> or you will descend through the roof
> with the spurious authority of a
> government official,
> blue as a policeman, grey as a used angel,... (*PP*, 30)

His beloved, however, enters wholeheartedly into his spatial assumptions about the world.

> Put down the target of me
> you guard inside your binoculars,
> in turn I will surrender
>
> this aerial photograph
> (your vulnerable
> sections marked in red)
> I have found so useful (*PP*, 37)

Much of the charm of this book resides in the woman's mocking use of the man's spatial aesthetics and in the frankness of her entry into a mutually exploitive relationship. He wishes to be a statue; she treats him like one. He acts insensitively, selfishly; she decides she can be equally happy with a useful corpse as with a sensitive lover.

> I approach this love
> like a biologist
> pulling on my rubber
> gloves & white labcoat
>
> ....
> Please die I said
> so I can write about it (*PP*, 10)

Here again a doubleness asserts itself. Games are sterile but fascinating; statues are cold but beautiful; illusionary order is false but addictive. The game of 'love' is exhilarating although not in any sense 'loving.' Beneath these various paradoxes lurks the central one of space subverted by time. "Power politics" for the persona is a children's game of pretense and fantasy. The book's verbal wit suggests the exhilaration of gamesmanship rather than the pangs of conscience. The self-irony suggests both the double vision of Susanna Moodie and a duplicitous 'procedure' for fantasizing away the processual underground.

The evidence of Atwood's first two books indicates that these considerations of the ethical dimensions of aesthetic systems have some bearing on Atwood's own aesthetics as a literary artist. In *Double Persephone* a direct link is visible between the formal garden inhabited by her personae and the formalism of the writing. Atwood exercises her own 'gorgon touch' here—substituting formal rhythms and language for the colloquial language of historical time, and replacing temporal characters with pastoral and mythological ones.

> The shepherdess with giddy glance
> Makes the amorous shepherd dance,
> While sheep hurtle the stiles for love
> And clouds pile featherbeds above;
> ("Pastoral," *DP*, 5)

In *The Circle Game*, a book with the thematic intention of discrediting the 'game' by which mankind converts time into space, the language is more casual and the surfaces of event, image, and characterization appear realistic.

> Love is an awkward work
>
> Not what I mean and
> too much like magazine stories
> in stilted dentists'
> waiting rooms.
> How can anyone use it?
>
> I'd rather say
> I like your
> lean spine
> or your eyebrows
> or your shoes
> ("Letters, Towards and Away," 70)

However, the 'underground' of the writing of *The Circle Game* is not the processual underground of the pioneer's farm—it is impersonal, mythological, and spatial. One notices this undercurrent in the first poem, "This is a Photograph of Me." The protagonist speaks as a dispassionate observer of herself. Presumably, she speaks from the temporal world beneath the surface of the photo and her detachment is only from the spatial world of the photographic image. But the aesthetic effect of the writing communicates detachment from both worlds: the language is factual, unemotional, the verbs are mostly ones of static condition, the concerns are spatial—where this persona is and of what size.

> I am in the lake, in the center
> of the picture, just under the surface.
>
> It is difficult to say where
> precisely, or to say
> how large or small I am (11)

At times in *The Circle Game*, the detachment from the self and from the human world in general is so complete that people are present only by synecdoche.

> The small carved
> animal is passed from
> hand to hand
> around the circle
> until the stone grows warm
> touching, the hands do not know
> the form of animal which was made or
> the true form of stone
> uncovered
> ("Carved Animals," 62)

Here, through both the synecdoche of "hands" and the passive voice of the opening verb, the sculptural reality of the carved animal is made dominant. The syntax of the poem, which alternates "hands" and terms for the "carved animal" ("stone," "animal") in the subject position, further dehumanizes the "hands" by making them appear parallel if not equivalent to the carved stone. The language also has a strong sculptural quality: the diction is factual and the rhythm dispassionate. By creating linguistically unlikely junctures away from the natural speech-pauses in the language, the line breaks enforce an unmodulated and non-colloquial tone. The temporal dimension of language as an emotional and personal response to experience is thus largely eliminated.

This tendency to embody a spatial aesthetic permeates all of Atwood's poetry. At the most elementary level, many of the central statements of her poems are assignations of relative spatial position. "I walk across the bridge...You saunter beside me,..." ("After the Flood, We," *CG*, 12). "In the background there is a lake, / and beyond that, some low hills... / I am in the lake,..." ("This is a Photograph of Me," *CG*, 11). "There is my country under glass,...and beside it 10 blownup snapshots..." ("At the Tourist Center in Boston," *AC*, 18). "When we were in it...now / we are out of it..." ("The Sunken Forest," *PU*, 18). Adverbial phrases of location play key roles in many of the poems: "kneeling on rock...above me...under my shadow" ("Dream: Bluejay or Archeopteryx," *PU*, 8-9); "under a tree... around you...on the other side...out of sight" ("Girl and Horse, 1928," *PU*, 10); "in this garden...outside the string borders...in the evening forest...in the bay...in another land" ("Two Gardens," *PU*, 16-17); "Upon the wall...around it...on the upper lip...on the skin" ("Projected Slide of an Unknown Soldier," *PU*, 46). Some poems combine such phrases with statements of spatial location to become entirely about relative spatial placement.

> Beside this lake
> ....
> my sister in bathing suit continues
> her short desolate parade
> to the end of the dock;

against the boards
her feet make sad statements
....
I sit in a deckchair
....
She moves the raft out
....
        The sun encloses
rocks, trees, her feet in the water, the circling
bays and hills...

(Under my hand the paper
closes over these
marks...

the words ripple...
towards the shore).
("Younger Sister, Going Swimming," *PU*, 66-67)

Somewhat more revealing is the repeated concern of many of the poems with making statements of condition. The underlying implication of such statements is the existence of static qualities—identity, colour, shape: "This is before electricity...the porch is wooden, / the house is wooden and grey;...("Game After Supper," *PU*, 7); "She is / a raw voice...She is everywhere, intrusive as the smells...immutable" ("The Land Lady,"*AC*, 14-15). This concern with establishing the essence of things is further indicated by the large numbers of copula verbs in Atwood, especially in opening lines: "Here there are no armies" (*PP*, 38); "You are / the lines I draw around you" (*AC*, 60); "The streets are new" (*JSM*, 50); "Marriage is not / a house" (*PU*, 60); "There are two of them" (*CG*, 68); "There are similarities" (*CG*, 57). In *Procedures for Underground* and the later collections most of the verbs are in the simple present tense and appear to indicate temporally uncircumscribed action.

> The sun shines down
>
> on two cars which have collided
> at a turn-off, and rest
> quietly on their sides
>
> and on some cows which have come over,
> nudge each other aside
> at the fence, and stare;
> ("The End of the World," *PU*, 32)

The static effect is amplified here and elsewhere by the selection of verbs denoting condition or minimal action—"shines," "rest," "stare," "refuse," "permit," "become":

> You refuse to own
> yourself, you permit
> others to do it for you:
>
> you become slowly more public: (*PP*, 30)

The temporal indeterminacy of such verbs can contribute to the creation of mythological or surrealistic effects:

> I keep my parents in a garden
> among lumpy trees, green sponges
> on popsicle sticks. I give them a lopsided
> sun which drops its heat
> in spokes the colour of yellow crayon.
>
> They have thick elephant legs
> ("Eden is a Zoo," *PU*, 6)

On other occasions this indeterminacy suggests habitual ongoing action and psychological estrangement from historical time.

I walk the cell, open the window,
shut the window, the little
motors click
and whir, I turn on all the
taps and switches

I take pills, I drink water, I kneel (*PP*, 19)

The result of such techniques is the removal of time as an operative dimension from much of the poetry. The speaker appears to be a spectator to her own life, standing outside both this life and its temporal context. The principle of cause and effect tends to disappear under such circumstances; events become juxtaposed in space rather than processually related. Such a condition prevails in "Progressive Insanities of a Pioneer" where the natural 'oceanic' action of the land is in no sense caused or precipitated by the pioneer who has juxtaposed himself to it. It prevails in "After the Flood, We," in which the two lovers are introduced syntactically as parallel subjects—"I walk across the bridge... you saunter beside me"—inhabiting parallel but self-contained experiences.

I walk across the bridge
towards the safety of high ground

....
gathering the sunken
bones of the drowned mothers

....
You saunter beside me, talking
of the beauty of the morning,
not even knowing
there's been a flood (*CG*, 12)

The syntactic parallelism is both ironic, in its implying the existence of a relationship that is etiologically non-existent, and real in specifying juxtaposition in space as the only operative link between its terms.

A similar lack of cause and effect prevails between the lovers of *Power Politics* whose relationship, despite their physical interaction, also appears to be one of spatial juxtaposition rather than of mutual causation.

> You are the sun
> in reverse, all energy
> flows into you and is
> abolished, you refuse
> houses,...
>
> I lie mutilated beside
> you; beneath us there are
> sirens, fires,...(*PP*, 47)

Here "you" and "I" are assigned parallel syntactic positions by the parallel syntax of "You are the sun" and "I lie...beside you." The spatial quality of the relationship is underlined by "beside" and "beneath"; the latter preposition joins the lovers to a list ("sirens," "fires") of spatially related objects.

This use of parallel syntax to indicate parallel but non-interlocking relationship is one of the principal technical resources of *Power Politics*.

> You say: my other wives
> are in there, they are all
> beautiful and happy,...
>
> I say: it is only
> a cupboard, my collection
> of envelopes,...
>
> In your pockets the thin women
> hang on their hooks...
>
> Around my neck I wear
> the head of the beloved,...(*PP*, 50)

In this instance the distinctness of the lovers is emphasized by the ironic contrast between the parallel syntax and non-parallel content. The woman's dialogue is a *non-sequitur* to the man's; the items "around my neck" are similarly irrelevant to the items "in your pockets." No temporal or causal relationship exists within either pair of items. The links are spatial: the juxtaposed lovers, their syntactically juxtaposed pronouns, their syntactically juxtaposed "pockets" and "neck," and the general juxtaposition created by the stanza arrangement. The overall effect is one of collage—collaged lovers, objects, and stanzas.

Atwood's recent work in *You Are Happy* shows little alteration in this manner of writing. A great number of poems are concerned with the making of statements of condition, in which verbs of action become indicators of states of being detached from temporal context.

> It is spring, my decision, the earth
> ferments like rising bread
> or refuse, we are burning
> last year's weeds, the smoke
> flares from the road, the clumped stalks
> glow like sluggish phoenixes....
> ("Spring Poem," 22)

When a first-person pronoun becomes a subject of these verbs, a self-detachment occurs in which the speaker seems to stand outside the atemporal frame in which the self exists and view this self as an object outside of process.

> History
> is over, we take place
> in a season, an undivided
> space, no necessities
>
> hold us closed, distort
> us, I lean behind you, mouth touching
> your spine,...
> ("Book of Ancestors," 95)

The very structure of many of the poems is spatial. Both sections and many stanzas in the multi-section poems ("Chaos Poem," "Tricks with Mirrors," "Four Auguries," "Head against White") appear to be in arbitrary sequence; no temporal logic would be offended by their rearrangement. Concluding lines gain their effect by the surprise of spatial juxtaposition rather than by temporal logic.

> overhead the weak voices
>
> flutter words we never said,
>
> our unborn children
> ("Useless," 10)
>
> ...I would wear them
> around my neck and pray to them
>
> like the relics of a saint,
> if you had been a saint.
> ("Digging," 19)

This structural technique resembles both that of modernist collage and that of the transcendence-seeking poetry of the early Imagist movement. The link between the juxtaposed elements is conceptual rather than temporal; their juxtaposition introduces juxtaposed contexts which propose an heuristic rather than causal relation.

> ...he slopes down,
>
> ....
> ...roped muscles leaping, mouth open
> as though snoring, the photography
> isn't good either.
> ("Newsreel: Man and Firing Squad," 8)

Atwood's use of personae in this book seems entirely designed to objectify conditions of being, to create a verbal sculpture of an abstract proposition. Such are the ten "Songs of the Transformed." The 'singers' all speak from outside themselves and regard their actions as repetitious, if not eternal.

> I crackle through your pastures,
> I make no profit / like the sun
> I burn and burn, this tongue
> Licks through your body also
> ("Song of the Fox," 40)

All have been, in fact, removed or "transformed" from time by human acts of mythology and stereotype.

The Circe persona in the long poem "Circe/Mud Poems" appears designed to stand in place of Atwood's own life on an Ontario farm and to 'transform' this life (much as the lives of the speakers in "Songs of the Transformed" have been transformed) out of its temporal context. The actual lovers become the mythological Circe and Odysseus, their farm becomes Circe's timeless island, their actual histories in time become the archetypal 'story' of immortal woman and mortal man. Circe here is another Medusa-Susanna Moodie figure who dislikes the timeless world in which she has lived. Her island seems to her a place of "ennui." Mythological men have become tiresome.

> Men with the heads of eagles
> no longer interest me
> or pig men, or those who fly
> with the aid of wax and feathers
>
> or those who take off their clothes
> to reveal other clothes
> or those with skins of blue leather

She seeks relief from both the unreality of such men and from the atemporality of her island.

> I search instead for the others,
> the ones left over,
> the ones who have escaped from these
> mythologies with barely their lives;
> they have real faces and hands,...(47)

Odysseus, on the other hand, despite his knowledge that it would be death to submit to transformation out of time, is still tempted by the timeless qualities Circe possesses. He becomes passive and quiescent.

> The trees bend in the wind, you eat, you rest,
> you think of nothing,
> your mind, you say,
> is like your hands, vacant: (50)

He relaxes into the deathly unrealities of mythological story.

> Don't you get tired of killing
> those whose deaths have been predicted
> and are therefore dead already?
>
> Don't you get tired of wanting
> to live forever? (51)

At times he seems to wish that Circe were not becoming alive, but would continue as a statue, a "woman constructed out of mud," one who "began at the neck and ended at the knees and elbows." Unlike a woman alive in historical time, such a statue would be "simple": "Is this what you would like me to be,/this mud woman? Is this what I/would like to be? It would be so simple" (61).

On the thematic level Circe succeeds in escaping into time. Odysseus' fear of transformation releases the talismanic fist from her neck (57), and she becomes aware of two possible "islands," one repetitive and timeless—"...the arrivals, / the bodies, words, it goes and goes, / I could recite it backwards" (67) —and the other in history, embodying events that have "never happened."

> The second I know nothing about
> because it has never happened;
>
> this land is not finished,
> this body is not reversible. (69)

At this section's conclusion she and Odysseus appear to walk on this second "island." Technically, however, the poem throughout is detached, sculptural, and spatial. Circe's consciousness is deliberate, self-detached, depersonalizing, and objectifying.

> We two eat
> and grow fat, you aren't
> content with that, you want more,
> you want me to tell you
> the future. That's my job,
> One of them, ... (66)

Even at the end of the poem where one is to assume she has returned to history, she speaks with a self-detachment that places her consciousness outside the temporal frame in which her body exists and which presents this body as principally an object in a spatial design.

> We lick the melted snow
> from each other's mouths,
> we see birds, four of them, they are gone, and
>
> a stream, not frozen yet, in the mud
> beside it the track of a deer. (70)

The theme of escape from space into time recurs in Atwood's work as frequently as events circle back on themselves in Circe's mythological home. From the Medusa of *Double Persephone* who yearns for a man who will resist her transforming gaze to the woman of the final poem of *You Are Happy* who sees her lover awaken from a sculptural pose, Atwood concerns herself with the tyranny of atemporal modes—mythology, stylization, ritual, cultural stereotype, commercial image, social manners— and with the contrasting richness of kinetic reality. Yet for Atwood, art itself inevitably seems to possess the 'gorgon' touch and works to transform life into death, flesh into stone. Almost all of her major personae are the artist-as-transformer: Medusa the statue-maker, the Power Politician who transforms her lover into a comic-book hero, Susanna Moodie who can remake her husband into her "idea of him" (*JSM*, 19), Circe who can make men into animals or "create, manufacture" hierarchic lovers (*YAH*, 47).

The struggle of these figures to abandon art and enter historical time is enlarged by the extra-temporal aesthetic implicit in Atwood's use of language and form into Atwood's personal struggle. In its own doubleness this struggle is impossible to resolve without her abandoning the practice of writing; it is therefore repeated in differing dramatic contexts from book to book. In each book, the language she employs communicates to the reader the presence of a consciousness divorced from the very temporal universe it argues he should enter. The reader thus experiences vicariously the dissociations from time and the detachment from being which the Circle Game or the game of Power Politics creates. The power of the poems is amplified by the implicit information in their language and form that the consciousness behind them suffers victimhood from the forces that the poems decry. Like Circe and Medusa, this consciousness has pathological power which it does not want, has insight into process and foreknowledge of event which only its alienation from process allows. Like a mirror, it creates art at the expense of its own participation in reality.

> Don't assume it is passive
> or easy, this clarity
>
> with which I give you yourself.
> Consider what restraint it

takes: breath withheld, no anger
or joy disturbing the surface

of the ice.
You are suspended in me

beautiful and frozen, I
preserve you, in me you are safe.

It is not a trick either,
it is a craft:

mirrors are crafty.
("Tricks with Mirrors," *YAH*, 26)

Throughout Atwood's work the operative irony is that a voice, excluded from time but wanting in, owes its very ability to speak to the static forms made possible by its exclusion. Art, speech, and writing are "crafty"; they separate one from process and from one's kinetic self. Her personae, as above, and elsewhere in *The Circle Game*. *Power Politics*, and Circe/Mud Poems, taunt their lovers with this knowledge. If these men wish to make use of the transforming power of the lady-artist, they must forego the temporal woman they may also desire. Atwood's poems circle back on themselves, recreating one central drama of artist-woman engaged in unsuccessful struggle to escape art for mortality. Essential to this drama is the implicit impossibility of resolution—an impossibility embodied in "the gorgon touch" with which Atwood's language, form, structure, and characterization are directed. Order here may conceal chaos, but only an embracing of order enables a speaking of either.

REREADING STEAD'S GRAIN

As Leslie Mundwiler's recent article, "Robert Stead: Home in the First Place," argues, the criticism of Robert Stead's fiction has been limited by an unstated assumption that a "faithfulness to reality is the main claim of Stead's work on our attention."[1] In some instances, Mundwiler notes, the assumption has been made during an attempt to identify Stead as a "realist" (Pacey[2]); in others it has underpinned thematic readings of Stead's novels as fictionalized accounts of social and economic history (Elder[3]). Mundwiler's article itself is a curious piece in that it devotes much of its length to detailing Stead's personal involvement in various public debates—the wisdom of government control of the grain industry, the effectiveness of Canadian copyright law, the hazards of monopoly-capitalism, the ominous penetration of U.S. monopoly into the Canadian economy, the tenuous future of Canadian books and magazines in a book industry increasingly dominated by U.S. publications—and yet argues finally that meaningful criticism must move past such details of his life and times to focus on "the concrete articulation of (the) narrative itself" and on "the active mythic force of language."

> Our response to novelistic narratives, which may be ignored in the process of assimilating the novel to scientific categories or platitudes, may challenge the very rules by which we expected to find it meaningful.[4]

As a textual experience, Stead's best-known novel, *Grain*, is indeed extraordinarily ambiguous. Certainly it provides at times a strong sense of 'realism,' but it provides so much in addition that realism is in no way its central effect. The opening chapter takes us quite another way. We are aware primarily of someone speaking, someone aloof and sardonic—a narrator, but one more concerned with presenting himself impressively than with objective narration. He has a story, and characters for this story, but is he interested in these characters or merely in displaying his own learning and wit by juxtaposing them to the characters?

> The eleventh of April, 1896, is not generally known as a date of special significance, yet it was on that day, or, to be more exact, that night, that the hero of this narrative made his entry into a not overhospitable world. Perhaps the term hero, with its suggestion of high enterprise, sits inappropriately upon the chief character of a somewhat commonplace tale; there was in Gander Stake little of that quality which is associated with the clash of righteous steel or the impact of noble purposes. Yet that he was without heroic fibre I will not admit, and you who bear with me through these pages shall judge whether or not the word is wholly unwarranted.[5]

Indeed, if we do bear with this voice and this narration, it is its own narcissism that has engaged us—its awareness of its own authority, its sense of personal superiority to the characters it is presenting, its pleasure in language skills beyond the reach of these characters, its amusement at the seriousness with which they regard their ostensibly minor lives.

> If he took note of his surroundings beyond the wooden cradle in which he lay, the arms in which he was lifted, the rounded founts from which he drew his nutriment, he must have marvelled at the habitation which Fate had selected for his home. To him at first it would seem very big, although his mother found it inconveniently small, and filled with equipment of amazing variety and interest. (17)

The 'high' language of these chapters—"special significance," "hero," "high enterprise," "righteous," "noble," "nutriment,"—implies a standard of judgement separate from the characters and events to which the narrator bears witness; cumulatively it operates as a critique of the characters which limits any identification with them. It is a language which excludes and judges them; they are privy neither to its vocabulary nor to the values the vocabulary signifies—a fact which Stead remarks on himself in the fourth chapter. Again speaking of his main character, young Gander Stake,

> He knew more than any of his teachers about the profession by which he was to make his livelihood, and he regarded book-learning as non-essential and irrelevant—neither of which words would he have understood. (40)

But these words are necessarily ones which both the reader and the narrator understand. This linguistic bond draws the reader to identify with the narrator—a narrator whose presence is indicated only by the language he uses—and not with characters whom this language appears to invest with realistic detail of action, reflection, and dialogue.

And yet this narrator does know the life of the pioneer farm, the speech habits of his 'commonplace' characters, the interiors of farm buildings.

> With an unreasoning disregard for the fitness of things, the early settlers always made use of shingle nails half an inch too long for the boards into which they were driven. It was the only shingle nail they knew, and that every nail should protrude through the board, splintering off a fragment at its end, they accepted as inevitable very much as they accepted early sunrise in summer and late sunrise in winter. In frosty weather each of these nail-ends became a condensing point for the household vapours, and a thousand little globules of ice formed in rows between the poplar rafters, dripping a little when the heat from the stove overpowered the cold at the other end of the nail, and recovering their losses through the long crackling night. (18)

But are these the objectivities of realism? Again Stead declares the narrator's superior perspective, attributing to the characters "an unreasoning disregard for the fitness of things." Again the diction and syntax are removed from the place they describe; the narrator's perspective eclipses the view of the Stake family of their own farm and encompasses all of pioneer life. The Stakes stand here as representative of "the early settlers"; the rafters, the stove, the "crackling night" are typical rather than particular; despite the detail, we are conscious not of standing close to the matter of the novel, as in realism, but further back with the narrator in a specifically developing viewpoint.

The exact nature of this viewpoint becomes visible slowly in these opening chapters, and is articulated not in the rhetoric of the narrative but in its imagery. It begins on the second page when Stead first attends to the animals and landforms among which Gander begins to grow. By the end of this page, the characters themselves are linked to animal life.

> Gander was utterly selfish....If he thought of his father at all he no doubt regarded him as an enormous, shaggy, but not dangerous animal, given at times to...unseemly curiosity concerning his—Gander's—toes, hair, and absence of teeth. The suspension bridge

> of scalp across a chasm in his little skull was a matter of concern to this great animal,...(16-17)

As soon as Gander can crawl, Stead follows him to the farmyard where Gander's true parents and siblings appear to be the farm animals— which Stead presents to us somewhat less condescendingly than he has the characters.

> He was fond of horses. He wandered among their feet at the peril of his life, but without mishap from that source. He was the foster-child of the family collie, Queenie, in whom he confided all his troubles and who was usually the first to locate him when he wandered too far from home. He hated geese, having had a disastrous encounter with that masculine bully of the farmyard from whom he was afterwards to derive his appellation; but he admired the turkey-gobbler, who strutted around with his great tail spread until it scraped along the earth and his bulging blood-red neck threatening instant apoplexy ...Ducks he loved. He would sit by the duck pond for hours watching them turn tail-up as they grubbed among the grassy roots, or filtering juicy morsels out of the water through their broad, chattery bills. With hens he had little concern. He regarded them somewhat as a small boy regards girls, as objects of slight interest and no possible importance. He liked his mother, tolerated his father, and hated his brother Jackson. But he loved Queenie. (20)

Gander's affinity with animals, and his implicit lack of affinity with humans, comes to us in numerous later passages. Interestingly, as the importance of the animals grows in Gander's life, the intrusions of the condescending narrator become fewer. Gander and the other children rush into their schoolhouse "'the way they load steers at the stockyard'"(31), at home Gander is "no more lonely on these prairies than is the coyote or the badger" (56), at church "his voice, unruly as any prairie broncho, plunged and bucked into unexpected and involuntary credenzas." When his voice goes "honking off over the heads of the congregation" (66), he acquires his nickname Gander.

The 'broncho' image of Gander engages Stead elsewhere when he describes the father as being "too wise a driver to let this colt feel the rein" (59), when he remarks that Gander's nickname is "as much his as though it had been branded on him with iron" (84), and when mid-way through the novel he tells of Gander's becoming "more than ever a creature of his father's farm," finding "companionship with his horses and machinery" (134).

By the sixth chapter the narrator is no longer a personality; Gander, meanwhile, has grown in definition—a 'groping,' pre-conscious, instinctual boy who has become sufficiently significant to the narrator to be written about directly, without irony or implied value judgement. Both the tone and situation are clearly more serious. Stead has shifted from mocking Gander to respecting him, and respecting him it seems because of his enmeshment in the ancient and unconscious patterns of biological process. The impression the language creates is that natural process has a dignity which is beyond mockery—whereas the Stake family's approximations of learning and 'heroism' do not.

> His mind was groping into new experiences, instinctively, but blindly...(63)

> ...Gander's attitude to Jo was too ill-defined to admit of very clear thinking. At school they had played together, preferring each other by some law of natural selection which neither understood nor tried to explain. (104)

The allusion to Darwinian 'law' in the second passage can scarcely be innocent, coupled with additional references to Gander's difficulty with "clear thinking" and understanding. Passages showing Gander in instinctual, reflexive responses now rise to our notice; earlier passages in which he suffered from maternal absence and diffidence, as when he "resented his mother's lack of enthusiasm" at his shooting his first goose (28), or when she "suppressed" "whatever sentiment or concern" she had felt on his return from his first day at school (39);

slightly later passages in which he experiences bitter feelings of sibling rivalry toward his brother Jackie who appears to be the mother's preferred son.

> ...he had no sympathy with her lamentations over his brother Jackie. Not that she often spoke of him; it was a name little heard in their household, but he seemed to be continually present in her mind, crowding from her life such happiness as she might have saved out of her drudgery. Gander thought this unreasonable. Jackie had gone—let him go. (113-114)

> ...he disliked Jackie. In childhood Gander had been the younger son, to be cuffed and ordered about by his big brother, and it was against his nature to take orders. And he was deeply attached to his father. Now Jackie would try to worm in between—(168)

The overtly Freudian character of Gander's anger toward mother and brother causes three other passages to carry particular significance. Perhaps two of these passages, relating the effect of the two hired men, Bill and Grit, on Gander's character, were written by Stead to show the influence of environment, and hence a further deterministic element in Gander's life beyond biology and instinct. Certainly they are the kind of passage that invites the assimilation to "categories" (the category here would be 'naturalism') which Mundwiler decries. But their effect for a reader is to more sharply define the depth of Gander's "resentment" toward his mother, and, even more important, to engage the reader's own Oedipal dramas. "It was Bill's theory that women are born to be mastered," Stead tells us, "that they recognize the master and obey him, but for those who are afraid they have only contempt" (67). Almost immediately Gander receptively mulls this idea over—"Girls love to be mastered" (68). Grit's ideas about women are equally hostile, but more disdainful than violent: "He regarded them from a distance, but with much quiet amusement. Women to him were like a picture show, to be looked at, laughed at, and forgotten" (140). In between these masculine examples we read of Gander's reaction to the suggestion of his girlfriend Jo Burge that "better men" than him have gone to fight in the world war—a reaction that brings to our minds both Gander's anger at women and the animal imagery through which Stead has viewed him.

> Something new had broken out in Gander. She read it in his eye, in the twist of his face, in the pose of his body like an animal set to spring. A horror of fear swept her. (131)

In this scene, a particularly upsetting one to the reader and to which he attends in some detail, Jo tries to run, but Gander pursues her—"a man she never had seen before, coming with slow menacing strides across the grass...Something wild had taken possession of him and egged him on in his madness." She runs quickly, but stumbles and falls, "motionless as death... a tiny trickle of blood...making its red way across her forehead." "In genuine alarm," Stead tells us, Gander carries her to a nearby pond; alarmed he may be, but he is also curiously pleased by his newly dominant role.

> She was light, but Gander was strong, and in memory he never knew whether she weighed more than a feather. Her head fell back, and was swinging free; he supposed that must be uncomfortable, and perhaps dangerous, so he raised her higher, and drew one of her arms about his neck. Her head now rested against his; he even could feel that trickle of blood against his cheek... (132-133)

The concluding ellipsis is Stead's, and reinforces the erotic quality of the scene for Gander. Jo's reaction as she regains consciousness is correspondingly one of a woman assaulted.

> 'Go 'way, go 'way!' she cried. 'Don't touch me! Go 'way!' There was such an abhorrence in her look that Gander shrank from it. 'I won't touch you,' he pleaded. 'But I'll help you home. You've been hurt.' 'Go 'way! Go 'way! I never want to see you again.

> I'm all right.' She rose unsteadily to her feet and drew her loosened skirt about her. (133)

The emphasis on "touch," "abhorrence," the "loosened skirt" makes this scene unmistakeably for us, Stead, and both characters, one of symbolic rape—the classic male expression of anger against woman. The usual components of the rape fantasy— the dichotomy of strong man versus fragile woman, eroticization of violence, and the male illusion of himself as rescuer—are all present. The latter was alive in Gander when first beginning his angry chase.

> ...even as he ran...he recalled that day [his first day at school] when he had rescued her, a little girl, from the prisoner's base and led her back triumphantly to safety. They had been friends then. They were friends yet. Of course they were friends. Of course. (132)

That this is the violent man's illusion the irony of the concluding "Of course" makes clear.

These three scenes—Bill's and Grit's advice, and Gander's 'assault' on Jo—clarify the exact range of Gander's resentment toward his mother and the dangers it constitutes to himself and the women he meets. Jo's response to Gander's hostility helps us to identify Bill's "theory that women are born to be mastered" as a rape theory, and to alert us to similar expressions of feeling later in the book. These scenes also provide the dark face of Gander's emotions toward his mother—an anger at her diffidence that corresponds to his unrequited yearning for her attention, a desire to wound that corresponds to an equally strong desire to nurture and protect, a desire to humiliate that corresponds to a desire to be held and comforted.

Curiously, the various Freudian dramas that we have in Gander's behaviour to this point have, despite their repugnant aspects, brought us very close to an identification with him. One reason for this effect is that since the sixth chapter (55-64) Stead's narrative intrusions into the text have been minimal, and our identification with a narrator has steadily weakened. In particular, we note few pejorative tones in the presentation of animal images or of family conflicts. Another reason seems to be the cumulative effect of the images and conflicts themselves, and their gradual engaging of feelings similar to those of Gander in ourselves. Gander's unconscious yearnings for a mother, and his fears of emotional barrenness in women, at times pervade even the descriptions of the landscape.

> ...the mocking tragedy of rain that threatens but does not come. It was though the heavens flirted with the earth, arousing her hope and passion, only to draw away in cold and beautiful disdain. (79)

Despite the sexual confusion in the pronouns of this passage, we recognize the earth's drama here as Gander's drama, and the heavens—cold, flirting, disdainful—as the image he projects onto all women. Jo Burge displays the same recognition in the lines that follow.

> 'I know—I know,' she murmured to herself. Then her sympathy suddenly mothered him. Riding close she threw her arms about him and kissed him on the cheek. The next moment she was galloping her cattle toward their own gate. (79)

The concentration of the imagery of the book on Gander, and of the action of the book on his relations with women, make Gander's feelings for Jo Burge overwhelmingly the core of *Grain* for any reader—despite the prominence given in various chapter openings to the historical forces of war and mechanization that frame the action. It is as though Stead himself, while initially believing himself to be writing a naturalistic novel of historical and biological determinism, found his own complex longings for the woman taking over the narrative—in Mundwiler's terms, found them challenging "the very rules" by which he "expected to find it meaningful." Moreover, Stead increasingly tends to see Gander's feelings as incestuous as well as potentially violent, and to make incest, specifically, a preoccupation of the book. Chapter by chapter, Jo becomes more linked in Gander's semi-conscious awareness with both his mother and his sister Minnie. His first romantic meeting with Jo is followed at once by a night storm during which Minnie, still a child, seeks warmth and reassurance in Gander's bed. He appears abruptly to resolve to give up his courtship of Jo, and while we do intuit the connection Gander is making, Stead significantly takes care to confirm it three chapters later.

> That spark [of desire for Jo] had been quenched, or at least subdued, by his curious reaction to the trust and hero-worship of his sister Minnie during the storm that night when they were alone in the house together. Gander was not a deep psychologist, but he had been unable to escape the conclusion that Jo was Tommy's sister just as Minnie was his sister. (104)

The delay of three chapters works to make the intuition our own, rather than that of Stead's narrator. The same subtlety in another link in the incest drama occurs in chapter 19, when Gander overhears his mother singing a lullaby to the young child Reed.

> ...one of the lullabies she had sung to Gander twenty years before. His Adam's apple had seemed to swell until it choked him at that sight. It tugged at something in his throat and whisked Joey Burge into his vision for a moment or two. (167)

This is a strong moment in *Grain*, profound and moving for writer as well as reader, and again highly suggestive of the force of Stead's engagement. Why it is Joey Burge who is "whisked" by the lullaby into Gander's vision Stead leaves for us to conclude—and we do.[6]

By chapter 19 several more years have passed, and when Gander again meets Jo it is

> ...no longer the child of his school days, the girl of his adolescence; this, beside him, was a woman, schooled in the responsibilities of the world, accustomed to facing difficulties without panic. She seemed to mother him now. (181)

We see Gander only now catching up to insights we have had about him for most of the novel. In fact, how explicitly Jo fills the role never accepted in his life by his mother, Gander is still not aware. We read this chapter's conclusion, particularly Gander's comments on Jo's invalid husband, with tender irony.

> ...how wise she was! She had set his mind at rest and filled his heart with a peace it had not known for years.
>
> 'And she's so good to Dick,' Gander commented, as he rehearsed their conversation.... 'She's a reg'lar mother to him.'
>
> A mother! Yes, that was what she was. Caring for her sick boy. But a wife? Gander wondered. (183)

It is Gander's growing discomfort with such a limited and psychologically taboo relationship with women that underlies the conclusion of the novel. It is a discomfort which the reader shares, and which makes the conclusion convincing by being welcome even if not totally plausible. In these final pages we see Gander with Minnie and then with Jo; both seem psychologically his mother, one "holding him in her arms" to give him melodramatic advice (205). There can be no satisfying sexual relationship here; we have known this since Gander first made the connection between Minnie and Jo during the storm of chapter 6.

There is no doubt in the final chapters what the novel is 'about'; it is about something more elemental than the issues of historical, environmental, or biological determinism that Stead earlier declared. It is about man and woman: man and mother, man and sister, man and wife. Gander's tragedy has been to be deprived of a mother by his family and later to be deprived of a woman—specifically, Jo Burge—by his continued unconscious search for a mother. One senses that even in the overtly naturalistic passages about the farm and its machinery Stead himself 'knew' this fact about his novel. The farm landscape is as much a maternal image as a deterministic one; Gander instinctively withdraws into it and 'feeds' from it, as if from alternate parents, even in childhood:

> ...he believed with our first parents that all the fruits of the field were given to man for his subsistence....He ate the leaves of every flower of the prairie, but was particularly partial to rose leaves and the purple blooms of the so-called prairie crocus. He gnawed the bark from the toothsome red willow, and he dug up 'snake' root and ate it moist and earthy as it came from its natural element. (23)

> After the first incident with Jo Burge, Gander became even more than ever a creature of his father's farm. He ploughed and harrowed early and late, and found his companionship with his horses and machinery. From even his father and mother he withdrew as into a shell. (134)

The farm machinery is sexual, rather than maternal—sexual for Gander in the excitement and energy it arouses in him, sexual for Stead also in the diction he uses to describe it.

> Gander drove up...the binder clattering as it came. The young teamster saw his father through the corner of his eye, and his chest swelled with manly pride. Not for an instant did he deflect his attention from the job at hand. He cracked his long whip over the backs of his four bays and they went on the half-run, the binder snapping out its great sheaves of golden wheat and its drive chain singing in the hot afternoon...the compressing finger came up; the cord tightened; the beak, with two threads of twine in its jaws, made the revolution, too quickly for the eye to see, and the knot was tied; the knife cut the string, and the sheaf fell on the carrier. Then the loose chatter of the packers as, the strain for the moment relieved, they thrust fresh wheat into the loop of twine left by the needle when it receded into its sheath. (44)

The details here are admittedly the matter of realism, but they are relentlessly glamourized by romantic diction and breathless, accumulating syntax, as Stead moves from Gander's chest swelling "with manly pride," to the "drive chain singing," "the strain relieved," the new "thrust" of the fresh wheat into the machine. In the scenes involving Gander's stoking of Bill Power's steam-driven threshing machine, the sexual overtones are even more explicit. The machine is clearly female. "'How's the old girl th' smorning?' Gander would say, as he raked the ash pan clean." Gander's role is of courtship in both act and setting. "Then came long minutes of gentle stoking, coaxing the fire to its maximum heat, and between times studying the stars or the waning moon." (99) When the machine is in full operation, it brings to both Stead's and Gander's minds an immediate comparison to Jo Burge.

> She was away! Gander let her ramble gently for a few revolutions while the exhaust beat its pleasant tattoo inside the stack, then slowly gave her more steam while he watched the quickening flywheel and knew the thrill that comes only to those who hold great power in the hollow of their hands. Jo Burge? This—this power—this mighty thing that sprang at his touch—this was life! (101)

In no other relationship in the novel is Gander so confident and alive, nor does he find any other love object this non-maternal and responsive.

That this is a limited "life" Stead was doubtless aware—witness his introducing very late in the novel the pastoral idea represented by the marriage of Minnie and Cal, an ideal involving not only education, wisdom, and a lakeside cottage, but an adult love as well. The example of Minnie and Cal, although involving stereotyped characters and a contrived twist of plot, at least underlines for us the barrenness of Gander's relationships. It underlines it for Gander himself, and awakens him to new possibilities for man-woman relationship beyond his own bitterness and the models of either his parents or of Jo and Dick Claus.

> In those days Cal and Minnie puzzled him a good deal. They were admittedly fond of each other. To be admittedly fond of a member of one's family had always been regarded by Gander Stake as a mark of weakness. (188)

He cannot overcome this puzzlement, however, and, like much else before, the sight of Minnie and Cal merely triggers his reflexive consideration of the futile mother-son dream incarnate for him in Jo.

> They [Cal and Minnie] would sit and look at the sunset on the lake with something in their eyes that puzzled Gander beyond words.
>
> Perhaps it was some of these things, or all of them, that turned Gander's thoughts, in spite of himself, toward Josephine Claus. (189)

Gander's problem—to find a way out of this dead-end existence in which women can only be enemies or mothers and in which sexual energy can be released only in the company of a machine —seems to become Stead's problem in the closing chapters, which is a remarkable reversal considering his condescension toward Gander at the book's beginning. Gander has evidently turned out to be more important to Stead than he believed him to be.

One idea Stead has insisted on throughout the book is that Gander is resistant to discipline—and no wonder, considering Gander's early lack of confidence in his parents. Stead appears to know that one trusts authority before obeying authority, and that the first authority for everyone is the mother —who here fails Gander in the matter of his first goose and leaves him to the affection of the family dog. Gander later is contemptuous of the obedient "form fours" soldiers "taking the lip of that fresh guy, and not saying a word back at him!" (125); he suffers "indignation" when a young woman advises him to take a job in the city—"All he saw was her attitude of superiority" (164). It seems he experiences some massive transfer of anger from his parents to any authority figure—even if she is as generous and attractive as the young woman here, Jerry Chansley.

A second idea which Stead had developed is that machinery is deathly as well as romantic—the metaphor of the binder harvesting a human crop on the battlefields of World War I (45, 91, 95) severely qualifies the 'romance' Gander finds in his machines, and suggests the emptiness of his fascination with them. The combined association of machinery with both sexual excitement and violence further associates it for the reader with the latent violence of Gander's feelings toward women—partly because these are the only instances of genuinely violent emotions in the novel.

In Jerry Chansley, Stead joins these two ideas to provide himself with a potentially hopeful conclusion. As Thomas Saunders observes in his introduction to the New Canadian Library edition, Jerry arrives too late in the book to be organic to its plot, and in this respect the conclusion is less than credible. But in terms of the two ideas above—that trust must precede discipline, and that pure machinery destroys the potential richness of human life, she is a quite logical development. Further, in terms of the increasing identification of Stead with Gander throughout the novel, Jerry represents an organic development indeed. That is, the resolution of Gander's difficulties with anger and resentment toward women, and of the paralysis these difficulties impose on his life, becomes in the novel an issue to which Stead personally appears to have an emotional commitment.

Jerry is unique to the novel in a number of ways—the only woman from the city, the only non-maternal woman, the only woman to have adult expectations of Gander, the only woman who can 'compete' with a machine, the only woman clearly associated with 'spontaneity' and freedom.

> ...something in that laughter had dug into strange, unused cells in his [Gander's] being. It was happy, spontaneous laughter—laughter without any ring of bitterness. When Gander laughed it always was in self-defence, as a mask behind which he could take shelter, or at the discomforture of some person or thing. Laughter was not much heard in the Stake homestead, and it nearly always was at people—not *with* them. This laughter was different, and it stirred Gander. (142-143)

Judging from the terms of the dichotomy here, Stead is stirred also. The second time we meet Jerry, it is through the windshield of Gander's car as she stands picking a flower in the grassy centre of the gravel road. We find that this time Stead has opposed her not to the untrusting Stake family but to the machine itself, her true sexual rival.

> ... Gander thrilled to the power of his car as it raced up the incline. As he swung over the top his brakes brought him up with a jerk. A few yards ahead a girl was bending over the grassy strip in the centre of the trail, in the act of picking some prairie flower which had braved the hazard of many horse's feet. The nose of the car was almost touching her when it stopped. (145-146)

For author and reader, this is an overtly symbolic scene. The machine, we see, is now both male and female, is simultaneously both Gander's 'thrilling' sexual partner and his own maleness—the phallic "nose" that almost touches Jerry before the car halts. This new ambiguity in the machine symbolism tells us something we should have guessed before—that Gander's fantasy sex-life with the machine has been essentially narcissistic, and in that sense homoerotic; that is, the machine to this point has served him as a medium through which he has been able to indulge and admire his own aggressive masculinity without having to resolve his relationships to actual women. But here the car, and its ambiguous thrill, are both at last stopped in their tracks by woman—a girl and a flower. Gander's reaction is his habitual anger. "'Well, I pretty near scored off you,' he said, annoyed that she made no move to get out of the way." Hers is "a ripple of laughter. It smote Gander like a blow. . . ." Like a blow because it is to him unprecedented, as are her "black hair," her "olive-brown skin," her "little black shoes," her "hands so small and fine"—all of which he suddenly begins to notice (146). Within minutes a strange event occurs—an animation in Gander we have not seen since his stoking of the steam engine. "Again she laughed, and Gander felt as though a short circuit were charging through his steering wheel." But surprise to Gander, and a relief to us, not from the machine. "No, it was coming from beside him; he knew it was coming from the passenger at his side. How dainty she was! How small, and how clean!" (147)

The next twenty pages are among the most disconcerting in Canadian fiction. Gander's animation is only a small spark, a spark of hope, certainly, to the reader, but one presently still dwarfed by his immense fires of rage and yearning. On leaving Jerry, Gander immediately begins to find his fascination with her intolerable. He feels humiliated, and has a brief rape-fantasy in which he unconsciously punishes her by envisioning her pinned beneath an overturned automobile and at the mercy of his physical strength.

> Absurd although it appeared, he gathered the idea that in some ways she was stronger than he. He almost wished that he had an opportunity to show his physical strength. If the car had turned over, for example. Suppose it had pinned her under! How he would have swung it up, his muscles knotted like iron! He would have raised her in his arms, he would have run with her to the nearest house. (150)

As in the rape-feelings Gander experienced earlier when carrying the unconscious Jo Burge to the pond, the woman is made weak by his strength, the sexual violence is disguised as 'rescue.' Moreover, the fantasy is his creation; it is his imagination which endangers Jerry in order to 'save' her. Within the fantasy he is himself the agent of her injury; it is his driving of the car, and *his* car (the car that she earlier stopped by standing in the roadway), that symbolically 'pins her under.' Out of guilt for his flash of unconscious sadism, a paragraph later Gander abruptly feels "a sudden surging in his heart toward his mother" and offers to help her as she plants young cabbages. Here is the yearning that underlies his rage. The mother is delighted "by this new experience," but also manages during the planting to comment that Gander "will never get in sight of that young minx" Jerry Chansley (151).

By the end of the next chapter, this suggestion that Gander is incapable of winning Jerry has become Gander's own conviction. He tells Jerry, "You think because you're from the city, an' have been to school more'n I have, an' wear fine clo'es, an' have pretty little clean fingers, I ain't good enough for you" (164-165). As he does so, he imagines that he sees "the figure of Jo herself... confusedly floating in and out between himself and Jerry," and finds himself re-enacting the sexual violence of his earlier fantasy.

> He had thrown an arm about her; he drew her slim body to his. He crushed her weak efforts, holding her fast, until his lips found hers. For a long time he held her. Life seemed to seep from her; her little frame went limp in his arms.
>
> With a sudden fear he let her sink in the grass and, turning, almost ran through the poplar groves to his own home. (165)

Clearly, given Gander's inner confusion about whom he is confronting —his mother, Jo, or Jerry, and his extraordinary swings between rage and yearning toward any mother-figure, Jerry is fortunate to come through this incident with her life.

The most bewildering aspect of *Grain*'s conclusion is not any change that occurs in Gander, and it is not Stead's belated introduction of new characters such as Cal and Jerry; it is Jerry's continuing patience with Gander. She writes to him from the city, her "you were very rude" (p. 177) being one of the mildest responses to a near-murder we can imagine. Jerry seems simply to refuse to believe Gander incapable of self-control, to refuse to believe herself endangered by him. She attends to some "sterling quality" in him (164), and matter-of-factly assumes its potential strength. Incredible? Perhaps so, but her expectations and her letter are nevertheless structurally essential for the story that Stead now wants to tell.

Her letter arouses complex reactions in Gander—and angry rationalization ("he had lost his head over her... but he had 'taken it out on her'") blaming her for his violence; his usual association of Jerry with Jo Burge; and, most important, a stirring "within him again of something he did not understand" (178). This "something he did not understand," ostensibly genuine (as opposed to violent) sexual feelings—elsewhere termed "a new revelation" (163), "a surging which he had no expression" (156), and a stirring of "unused cells of his being" (142)—is again no less than the spark of hope on which Gander's future rests. It is also the spark of hope on which Stead gambles the end of his novel, introducing Cal to fan it by example and Jerry to awaken and re-awaken Gander to its presence.

The concluding chapter greets us as a tug-of-war between these new responses in Gander, represented by Jerry Chansley, and the older, hopeless, and potentially incestuous yearnings represented by Jo Claus (both, as Gander recognizes, bearing the initials 'J.C.'). Jerry's letter stays in his coat pocket, emerging occasionally to tempt him with the future.

> With something akin to a great tenderness he drew the note from its battered covering, and spelled it out again in the mauve light which flowed up from the lake in reflection to the sky overhead. Yes, Jerry had been a strange but tender incident in his life. She must have cared for him a little, at least, or she would not have written that note. Perhaps, even yet—(201)

Jo, sadly determined to "serve" her permanently invalid husband "to the end"(194) yet seemingly sexually open to Gander, offers Gander another of the ambiguous and partial relationships he has experienced since birth. The latter is a relationship that still feels to us as much incestuous as adulterous—a relationship to the sister of his dead friend Tommy Burge, to the wife of his other friend Dick Claus.

A lot has occurred in the narration between this chapter and the book's beginning. The supercilious narrator has vanished, the typological descriptions of the Stake family as representatives of prairie life have vanished, the imagery of historical, environmental, and biological determinism has dwindled, and the passages of detailed realism have ceased. The orderly and realistic unfolding of plot has been broken by the gratuitous introduction of new characters. The very title of the book, *Grain*, with its connotations of the implacable man-dwarfing processes of season and harvest, is changed by Stead abruptly in this last chapter into a humanistic symbol, when Minnie describes Gander's pending choice between Jo and a new job in the city as a choice between the chaff and "a little hard yellow golden grain . . . the essence of life, Gander" (204).

Grain is by now the story of a narrative as much as the story of Gander Stake, a narrative to which we must attend and respond, as Mundwiler argues. It is the story of a novelist who began to care for his main character, to identify with him before even the mid-point of the novel, losing his initial amused detachment from him, losing his will to see him as a mere pawn of deterministic forces. The story of a novelist who cares so deeply for his main character that he breaks with credibility to introduce in the concluding chapters new characters and a pastoral, anti-realistic, subplot, to give this character some faint hope in the novel's last pages.

"I could have killed you," Gander tells Jerry when she stands in the roadway in front of his car. And he could have, on at least one more occasion as well, and could certainly have 'killed' in a number of ways his own chances in life. But curb our 'naturalist' expectations. Stead will not let Gander be a McTeague, and so goes through the modes—irony, realism, naturalism, pastoral, romance—to release Gander from this probability. And repeats the phrases of hope—the "unused cells," the "stirrings" for which he has "no expression." And finally makes the one act which has been impossible for Gander, the accepting of discipline through the granting of trust, paradoxically the way by which his freedom from naturalistic determination is to be achieved and the "unused cells of his being" set in motion. The trust here on the book's last page is significantly not the child's trust in the mother but the adult's trust in himself. "'Gander,' he said at length, 'now you will take your medicine, and you will take it from yourself.'" The new assumption of adulthood is signalled further by the note he now writes to Jo, telling her of his decision to leave immediately for the city. "He was about to sign it 'Gander,' but a sudden dignity was upon him. He inscribed his initials, W.H.S." (207)

It has been Stead's gift to Gander of Jerry Chansley that has allowed him this moment. For Jerry has given Gander not only an offer of a job in the city but also a new view of himself as a "serious" person. She has dealt with him as an adult capable of overcoming mechanistic and biological force. When he tells her, "I could have killed you," she replies "Oh, you are much too good a driver to do anything like that." When she advises him to take a job in the city, and go back to school as well, Stead takes pains to underline her "seriousness" and to apologize for Gander's angry reaction: "Gander was too inexperienced to appraise that seriousness at its real value." It is a seriousness we see Gander having internalized on the last page when he signs his adult initials and accepts his responsibility to life's "muddy road" (207). It is a seriousness also that Gander, despite his inchoate fears and anger, has always wanted for himself, hoping to be called 'Bill' by his father (61), eager to assume "a man's life" (59) beside his father in the farm work.

And so Stead has moved himself and us from literary determinism to individual responsibility, from naturalism to romance, from entrapment in Freudian drama to a quest for a Maslowvian grail. Has moved us, that is, if we have attended to the narrative, its accumulations of significant image and incident, its breaking of the expected "rules," its evading of the literary categories. Gander will probably not win Jerry—the likelihood of his quickly outgrowing his enormous hostility to women is minimal—but he has chosen to pursue the maturity she embodies. His choice of the city is a rejection of the maternal woman, an affirmation of his own self-worth, and a decision at least to question his feelings of rage. The overall movement of the novel is a persuasive one, because of Stead's palpable fondness for Gander, because of the "unused cells" of response in Gander, and because of our own yearnings for such a state of being as Jerry represents. Jerry herself, despite her necessary one-dimensionality, her daintiness, her small fingers, we experience as no cliché heroine but as a symbolic composite of adult values calling us away from the mother's house, the maternal landscape, the barren excitement of machines, and toward a real sexuality beyond "the muddy road."

---

1. *Essays in Canadian Writing* 11, Summer 1978, p. 198.

2. "Fiction 1930-1940," in Carl F. Klinck et al., ed., *The Literary History of Canada*, 2nd ed., Vol. II (Toronto: University of Toronto Press, 1976), pp. 186-188.

3. "Western Panorama: Settings and Themes in Robert J. C. Stead," *Canadian Literature* 17, Summer 1963, pp. 45-56.

4. Mundwiler, p. 199.

5. (Toronto: McClelland & Stewart, 1963 [1926]), New Canadian Library, no. 361, p. 15.

6. Since publishing the present essay in *Studies in Canadian Literature* IV:1 (Winter 1979), I have discovered a lengthy paper by Gordon Turner, "The Incest Bond in Stead's *Grain*" (*The Sphinx* II:3 [Winter 1977]) with which I would have taken issue had I seen it earlier. Turner focusses on the storm scene in which Minnie huddles with Gander in his bed, and mistakes it as representing an actual "incestuous bonding" for Gander which recreates "the comfortable retreat of childhood." My reading here has been that Gander experiences Minnie not as a sister but as a mother; the scene causes him to lose interest in Jo Burge not because of an "incestuous bonding" to Minnie but rather because of its reminding him of the taboo quality of his attraction to Jo as a mother-surrogate. Turner's interpretation of the incest 'bond' in *Grain* as a brother-sister one is in my view superficial in both its psychological reading of the relationship between Gander and Minnie and in its failure to note Stead's emphasis on the mother role both Minnie and Jo play in Gander's mind throughout the novel.

THE EXPLORER IN WESTERN CANADIAN LITERATURE

The first fact we notice in this territory is how infrequently the names of the historical explorers occur. When we do encounter them, it is their limitations, their disappointed expectations, that have engaged the writer. We find Newlove's Samuel Hearne, shaken by the cold and filth of the northern landscape yet finding this cold "impossible to describe," and himself, when his Indians guides execute an Eskimo girl, "helpless before his helpers." [1] We see Birney's Captain Cook sailing

> north from the Golden Gate
> to where nothing was certain on the maps
> except that lance-straight giant's channel
> cleaving the continent from Brobdingnag
> to Hudson's Bay and home

He encounters only

> ...kelp snakes
> writhing ship-long on the water
> a coast coldly smoldering
> Over the drowned peaks heaved the seals
> Land was a meaningless tramping of trees
> a pike-staffed army pacing them all summer

The words tell us of a landscape that is angry, dangerous, and much larger than Cook's ability to ascribe meaning. The one "lance-straight" reality he encounters is ironically not the Strait of Anian which he expected but the Hawaiian spear in the back which sends him "to explore his last reef."[2] We are given the explorer as corpse, and given thereby a large hint about the futility of his earlier explorations.

This picture of the explorer as someone divorced by expectations from reality we find also in George Bowering's long poem *George, Vancouver,* a poem which considers both Cook's explorations and Vancouver's attempts to confirm and enlarge them—although here the responsibility for the explorer's illusory goals is placed by Bowering on George III rather than on Cook and Vancouver themselves.

> It was the king's fancy that Cook's "River" was the passage across British North America that would allow him to send his fighting men to the Pacific to defend his interests.
>
> Captain Vancouver found that the River was just an inlet, & so it was renamed Cook's Inlet.
>
> Captain Vancouver's botanist, Menzies, spent his time finding & describing new plants on the Coast.
>
> The Indians weren't asked what they thought about the Anglicans, so they never discoursed on the relationship between fancy and the real.[3]

Like Birney, Bowering sees Cook, together with George III, as preoccupied with 'fancy'—the king's belief in the Strait of Anian—and therefore unprepared for the living landscape, which again is too complex and fluid for him to encompass.

> To chart this land
> hanging over ten thousand inlets
> and a distant mind of as many narrows,
>
> an impossible thing—
> no music
> sounds as many changes with such
> common theme.[4]

Both Birney and Bowering imply a distinction between the quester and the explorer, between one who seeks confirmation of preconceived idea and one who seeks to experience "the real." Bowering uses both Vancouver's meeting in Nootka Sound with the Spanish explorer Quadra and the sexual dimension of the Strait of Anian image to signal the need for the explorer not to be the questing knight of the grail legend.

> The soft air of the inland sea
> & heaving spray in the dark spruce
> offer no grail, it was no grail
> he was after, he was not
> sailing with that kind of purity.
>
> He stopped to dine on the silver plates
> of the Spanish, Quadra saw no
> Celt there, but Vancouver, the reformed
> Dutchman, a young sailor
> with an appetite.[5]

The real for Bowering is what is discovered rather than sought, it is sexual and botanical rather than conceptual. The only grail or Strait of Anian that Vancouver enters is in making love to an Indian woman who welcomes him "like an inlet / of warm water." The other successful explorer of his expedition is his botanist, Robert Menzies, a man who "never thinks / about the king's / northwest passage," who instead "pulls the weed out of the ground / to poke around at its roots,"[6] and produces drawings of Indian weeds which are "some surety, an illustration of a leaf / with only a thousand lines in it."[7]

The myth that arises in these poems is of the power and mystery of the land that resists "Romance" in Newlove, "certainty" in Birney, and human "fancy" in Bowering. Concurrently the poems imply as false myth the explorer as would-be Parsifal, exploration as quest-romance, landscape as holy-grail. Within these poems there is a collision between European tradition and expectation and North American landscape, between Brobdingnag and the drowned peaks of the northern islands, between the romantic image and human manure, between the Strait of Anian and Cook's Inlet reproduced in Vancouver's meticulous chart-making on the cover of *George, Vancouver*. Implicit is the idea that the land is massively more important and vital than its explorer—an idea which perhaps explains why in all the landscape-rich work of Laurence, Wiebe, Livesay, Marlatt, Lane, Mitchell, Ross and Grove so little mention of early exploration is made. As in Birney's "The Mammoth Corridors," the geologic extravagances of "howling summits" and "fresh-hewn alps" dwarfs

> ...those first compulsive whites the Searchers
> for gold absolution furs or mere difference
> [who] came hurtling in improbable canoes heavy with liquor
> muzzleloaders and god.[8]

Implicit also is the question of who the explorer is, or should be: a Parsifal or an Odysseus, a quester or a "sailor / with an appetite." We find an objection to goal-directed exploration, the search for gold, for an overland route to the Pacific, for furs, for the Strait of Anian, and by further implication to Columbus' quest for the Indies or Franklin's for the northwest passage. In the major western treatment of the Odysseus story, Kroetsch's *The Studhorse Man*, Hazard Lepage's quest to breed the perfect horse is viewed as absurd and mistaken—a refusal, as Ann Mandel has argued, of the body, of life, of sexuality, as well as death, and overall a parody of Odysseus' wanderings.[9]

Latent within these various accounts of wrong-headed, goal-oriented exploration would seem to be an assertion of the Odyssean wanderer as the better model. The clearest examples of such an assertion are Kroetsch's novels, particularly *Badlands*, a novel specifically about exploration. The protagonist, William Dawe, leader of the William Dawe Expedition into the Alberta Badlands in search of museum-quality dinosaur skeletons, is a quester—an Orpheus whose Eurydice is his fantasized Daweosaurus which he dreams of retrieving from his Badlands descent.

> From seventy million years deep in the black matrix of the past the bones must leap to light. Must loose themselves from the bentonite. Must make their finders rich and famous. The bone that must satisfy their finders.[10]

Dawe's determination to make the past live is a denial of death, a denial of the contemporaneity of his own sexuality, and a rejection of the woman who offers herself to him; it renders him "indifferent to all the real and natural world."[11] His particular grail, or in Bowering's terms, his 'fancy,' is history; it is history, things which have died, which obsesses him and blinds him to the human present. Yet paradoxically it is not his questing will which allows him his three discoveries of the past; it is the accidents of the unstructured and appetite-directed present. He discovers his first skeleton as a result of a visit by one of his workmen to a whiskey-still; the second through looking for a shortcut back to camp while thinking wistfully of his Ontario wife; the third through his Indian mistress' stumbling upon it while fornicating with another man in a thunder storm. The message is that successful exploration requires what William Dawe most lacks—a quick responsiveness to event, openness to experience and sexuality. Instead Dawe stubbornly remains committed, in his daughter Anna

Dawe's words, to "shutting out instead of letting in";[12] and in his mistress Anna Yellowbird's more graphic words—which also invoke Birney's contrast in scale between nature and man—to "pissing in the ocean." Ultimately, the true explorers in *Badlands* are not any quest-driven men but the two Annas with whom the book ends, who hurl William Dawe's field notes and photographs into a lake, and who refuse "dinosaurs or men or their discipline or their courage or their goddamned honour or their goddamned fucking fame or their goddamned fucking death-fucking death," who refuse to "look back, not once, ever."[13]

In these women we see again the counter-myth of the explorer as receptive adventurer. Their forerunner in Western Canadian fiction is Topaz Edgeworth of Ethel Wilson's 1949 novel *The Innocent Traveller*. In this recounting of the emigration of three elderly British women to Vancouver in the late nineteenth century, we find Topaz part of another contrast between preconception and reality—as when her older sister becomes upset by the very concept of a buffalo, and relieved to see Ontario sheep grazing "in an international manner."

> They did not seem to know or care they were Canadian sheep and should perhaps behave differently in a characteristic way, like the bison. They might indeed have been sheep of Staffordshire. Neither were the cows different from the English beasts in their behavior, the dear familiar cows.[14]

Topaz, who has been the one who troubled her sister by her enthusiastic account of the bison, also upsets her by exploring the gentlemen's smoking-room on the train and claiming that in Canada one has to be prevented by the porter at each stop from naively "getting off the train to 'walk upon the prairie.'"[15]

In all these works exploration becomes a metaphor for life and, by implication, for the writing process itself. Newlove, Birney, and Bowering all juxtapose the explorer's world with the twentieth century and with their own lives. In "Samuel Hearne in Wintertime," Newlove sees his own sick children as embodiments of the sickly Indian children Hearne saw in the winter encampments, and both situations as calling on man to do more "than endure." In *George, Vancouver* the title simultaneously denotes the explorer, the tensions between George III and the explorer, and the presence of the poet, George Bowering, in the city Vancouver. The exploration is concurrently Vancouver's of the lower B.C. coast and Bowering's of both that exploration and of the nature of exploration itself. The final poem reads as both Bowering's and Vancouver's: "Let us say / this is as far as I, George, / have travelled."[16]

Birney's "The Mammoth Corridors" makes no distinction between "those first compulsive whites" and the contemporary skid-road businessmen—"the spastic traffic / of buyers and bought pedlars of weed and soap / of acid and snow of work and wonder / in skidrow's lanes."[17] And in "Pacific Door" Birney recalls "dying Bering lost in fog" and "Drake's crewmen" who "scribbled here their paradise," and then proposes the ineffectuality and isolation of the explorer as symbolic of the limitations of a race:

> Here Spaniards and Vancouver's boatmen scrawled
> the problem that is ours and yours
> that there is no clear Strait of Anian
> to lead us back to Europe
> that men are isled in oceans or in ice
> and only joined by long endeavour to be joined.[18]

For Kroetsch and Wilson also the explorer embodies the problem of how to live—innocently or cautiously in *The Innocent Traveller*, openly or narrowly in *Badlands*. The goal of 'exploration' for these novelists is not merely Newlove's of "Samuel Hearne in Wintertime," "to know," or Bowering's of *George, Vancouver* to make "the eye's charter, the diary of Menzies, botanist, illustrator, practical man, curious,"[19] but impulsiveness and laughter. All five writers see the explorer as an artist whose works vary in quality with the openness of his methods. In the first chapter of *The Innocent Traveller*, Topaz as a young child is already the family poet, irrepressibly reciting her verses to the visiting Matthew Arnold, and infuriating her businessman father with both her poems and her gay description of the family's new water closet. William Dawe for Kroetsch is the anti-artist, obsessed with recovering and rebuilding the past to the exclusion of the living present so real to Wilson's Topaz. Both Bowering and Newlove, by identifying their circumstances with those of Vancouver and Hearne, make the explorer's task a metaphor for that of the writer, for Newlove that task becoming "to know, to do a job,"[20] for Bowering the "trusting" of oneself "to the Inland Sea/forgetting stories of the Strait of Anian,/ setting foot among actual salmonberries."[21] Bowering in fact subtitles *George, Vancouver* "a discovery poem."

Not surprisingly, exploration is also a metaphor in much west-coast aesthetic theory, particularly in Newlove, Bowering, and Daphne Marlatt. Newlove writes: "Ride off any horizon/ and let the measure fall/where it may"[22] and with the pun on "measure" links the explorer's chart to the poet's line. The explorer is mapmaker, as the cover of Bowering's *George, Vancouver* reminds us, and Bowering in a recent interview remarks that poetry is "trying to find out where you are." Referring to his use of the term 'locus,' he says, "It implies I'm trying to locate myself."[23] Marlatt, in commenting on her book *Rings*, describes it as an act "of charting a territory that was unknown, that I find myself in, and having to map it out to discover who I was."[24]

Much of Marlatt's use of exploration as a metaphor for art involves what we might call temporal mapping. In *Badlands* two of Kroetsch's explorers were inadequate because they ignored time —Dawe by trying to preserve the dead, the photographer Sinnott by photographing the "vanishing" instant. A third, the minor character Web, has the correct theory but even while theorizing cannot act upon it.

> There was no past, never. He would not let go, remembered with long deliberation the endless swoop and marvel of swallows...; gone now. Time. Remembered the last cactus....[25]

As if responding to Kroetsch, Marlatt says photographs "are unreal because the real is the constant streaming of time, and they try to take a fix on it."[27] And as if responding to Bowering's and Birney's criticisms of Cook's expectations of a Strait of Anian, says

> The trouble with consciousness is that it gets tied up in the world. Which means that you're willing how things are going to turn out. Which means that you're cutting out...most of the field that we're involved in...you can put it in electromagnetic terms: we're under an electromagnetic grid which we aren't even aware of most of the time. But it's the very basis for everything that comes in. I'm trying to be as aware of all that I'm in the midst of as I can.[27]

In Marlatt's major 'exploration' poem, *Steveston*—another book with a map on its cover—it is not just place but time and place, or place in time, which are to be explored and mapped.

> ...Driving lines that shift, the floor does, ground or
> under sea, to cast, at low tide what lies uncaught, uncovered
> traces only, of sun & the moon's pull.
> Unseen, how lines run
> from place to place,...
>
> But the place itself, mapt out, a web, was grass:
> tall, bent grass swaying heavy with seed. Cottonwood whose
> seeds make a web in the wind....[28]

The inhabitants of *Steveston* become implicit explorers because moment by moment geography changes as the sandbanks shift, the winds rise, the seas roll.

> In gumboots
> on deck with rubber apron ('it's no dance dress'), she'll take
> all that the river gives, willing only to stand her ground (rolling,
> *with it*, right under her feet, her life, rolling, out from under,
> right on out to sea...[29]

The model that emerges from these works is of an explorer or artist who is engaged not in history or in an anticipated future but in Marlatt's "continuous present"; who works not with design or premeditation but in response to what is encountered— Newlove's letting "the measure fall/where it may"; who interacts with shifting "ground." It is the model provided by Kroetsch's Anna Dawe and Anna Yellowbird discarding the fifty-six-year outdated photos and field notes to "stumble" their own "way by the light of the stars."[30] Throughout, the implications for form— structure, simile, metaphor, symbol—are that it is to be stumbled upon like the two Annas' future. Marlatt has articulated this view particularly clearly—first speaking of simile and metaphor, "We don't get similes, we don't get those laid-on metaphors but rather the discovered ones in rime...And etymology."[31] And then speaking of structure,

> I've often had a feeling when I'm writing that it's like trails through the woods, & that there are all these branching-off places, & some of these simply peter out. They don't get anywhere, so then you have to backtrack. That's when you delete & edit, because you realize, okay, that's a dead-end, & those are traps. I really believe that you can't get straight from here to there; you have to in some way be led. But you never know if what's leading you isn't going to lead you to a dead-end, so you have to be watchful.[32]

Bill Bissett has argued similarly for a process of composition that is more a mapping than a construct of fancy.

> each pome has within its happening its own ordering
> its own rule sometimes evn takes thru a lot uv trubul to make it...
> look like what it is, its energy transmittid without any forcing
> that isn't in the pome.[33]

Of symbolism, Robert Kroetsch tells us, "...you have to work from your observed, literal world. You can't go through after [,] putting in the symbols."[34]

Certainly in these writers there is a strong sense that the explorer metaphor for the writer has become internalized, often both in terms of exploring experience and exploring language. Terms such as *mapping, discovering, grounds, lines, trails* have become part of the aesthetic vocabulary. The map on the cover of the book—as in *Steveston, George, Vancouver,* Roy Kiyooka's *Trans-Canada Letters,* Gerry Gilbert's *May 1931*—becomes a metaphor in turn for the accuracy aspired to by the text within. Many of the texts—notably Marlatt's *Steveston* and *Zócalo,* Kroetsch's *Stone-Hammer Poems,* Bowering's *Autobiology,* Gilbert's *Journal to the East,* Andreas Schroeder's *File of Uncertainties,* J. Michael Yates' "Hunt in an Unmapped Interior" and *Great Bear Lake Meditations,* and Newlove's "Crazy Riel"—claim the unconditioned structure of the journal or ship's log, or of ongoing recollection, or even of speech made to fill silence. In Marlatt's work, in addition, we encounter a shifting plurisignative syntax that corresponds to the shifting 'grounds' (*Rings*' "our grounds, even the grounds dispersed,"[35] *Steveston's* "lines that shift, the floor does, ground or under sea,"[36] "persistent bending windswept lines of force,"[37] "town down stream in its own downpour"[38]) that the experiences rest on.

Further examination of the texts to determine the extent of realization of these structural and sometimes syntactic principles is outside the scope of this paper. What is clear is that from Earle Birney and Ethel Wilson to the present, the explorer as chartmaker and wanderer has engaged the Western Canadian literary imagination—to the point of becoming a metaphor for the writer. In such metaphor the explorer represents not only an accurate responsiveness to experience but also the immense and creative force of the grounds, lines, tides, and winds which limit his 'fancy' and will.

---

1. "Samuel Hearne in Wintertime," *The Fat Man* (Toronto: McClelland & Stewart, 1977), p. 61.

2. "Captain Cook," *Selected Poems* (Toronto: McClelland & Stewart, 1966), pp. 4-5.

3. (Toronto: Weed/Flower Press, 1970), p. 7.

4. p. 5.

5. p. 39.

6. p. 26.

7. p. 5.

8. *Rag and Bone Shop* (Toronto: McClelland & Stewart, 1971), p. 12.

9. "Uninventing Structures: Cultural Criticism in the Novels of Robert Kroetsch," *Open Letter* (Third Series), no. 8 (Spring 1978), pp. 52-71.

10. (Toronto: Paperjacks, 1975), p. 31.

11. p. 56.

12. p. 269.

13. p. 270.

14. (Toronto: Macmillan, 1949), pp. 110-111.

15. p. 115.

16. p. 39.

17. *Rag and Bone Shop*, p. 11.

18. *Selected Poems*, p. 142.

19. p. 30. We note that "curious" later becomes the title of another Bowering book in which he explores his images of contemporary Canadian and U.S. writers.

20. *The Fat Man*, p. 63.

21. *George, Vancouver*, p. 15.

22. "Ride off Any Horizon," *The Fat Man*, p. 41.

23. *Outposts*, ed. Caroline Bayard and Jack David (Erin, Ont.: Press Porcepic, 1978), p. 79.

24. "Given this Body," interview with George Bowering, *Open Letter* (Fourth Series), no. 3 (Winter, 1979). p. 63.

25. p. 235.

26. "Given this Body," p. 46.

27. p. 42.

28. (Vancouver: Talonbooks, 1974), p. 85.

29. p. 75.

30. *Badlands*, p. 270.

31. "Given this Body," p. 43.

32. p. 50.

33. *Outposts*, p. 63.

34. "A Conversation with Margaret Laurence," in Robert Kroetsch, ed., *Creation* (Toronto: New Press, 1970), p. 58.

35. (Vancouver: Georgia Straight Writing Series, 1971).

36. p. 85.

37. p. 86.

38. p. 48.

LADY ORACLE'S SECRET: ATWOOD'S COMIC NOVELS

When Margaret Atwood's *Surfacing* appeared, I wrote that it seemed to be a reworking of her first novel, *The Edible Woman.*[1] "In each a young woman of some sensitivity finds herself alone among predominantly form-asserting and exploitive people," I said. "In each the young woman's body realizes the threat which these people and their way of life constitute to her integrity well before her mind can gain a corresponding insight. Their bodies both attempt to take over leadership of the whole woman in order to bring her to knowledge and safety. They attempt flight, they refuse food, they prohibit certain activities. A kind of madness thus seizes the young woman, a madness in which her new pre-conscious and body-dominated perspective makes everyday events become frighteningly surrealistic. Her images of reality here are prelogical, discontinuous, yet carry an uncannily convincing symbolic truth. In *The Edible Woman*, the girl's fiancé attempts to photograph her:

> That dark intent marksman with his aiming eye had been there all the time, hidden by the other layers, waiting for her at the dead centre: a homicidal maniac with a lethal weapon in his hands.

In *Surfacing* a group of friends and acquaintances attempts to 'rescue' her from her apparent insanity and return her to 'normal' city life:

> They're hulking out of the boat now, four or five of them. I can't see them clearly, their faces, the stems and leaves are in the way; but I can smell them and the scent bring [*sic*] nausea, it's stale air, bus stations, and nicotine smoke, mouths lined with soiled plush, acid taste of copper wiring or money. Their skins are red, green in squares, blue in lines, and it's a minute before I remember that these are fake skins, flags.

In each case the onset of the madness results in the narrative switching from first-person viewpoint to third person in relating her story. In both cases when the young woman does achieve some conscious insight into her self and its situation, the body can relinquish its usurped powers to a somewhat reintegrated being. Finally, at the moment of insight each young woman comes to view her problem symbolically as a dissociation of body from head."[2]

In 1976, on reading Atwood's third novel, *Lady Oracle*, I was again aware immediately of resemblance to the earlier fiction. Another young woman so detached and alienated that she experiences friends, parents, husband, as utter strangers. Another narrator who, overwhelmed by the dangers and complications she perceives around her, escapes, if not into madness at least into a 'mad' act of feigned suicide and uncomfortable exile. Another narrator who learns enough during her 'exile' to drop her paranoia and attempt again some contact with the human world she has fled.

•

In both her 1972 interview with Graeme Gibson and her 1976 interview with Linda Sandler, Atwood took pains to classify both *The Edible Woman* and *Surfacing* as "anti-comedies." She explained to Gibson,

> ...in your standard 18th-century comedy you have a young couple who is faced with difficulty in the form of somebody who embodies the restrictive forces of society and they trick or overcome this difficulty and end up getting married. The same thing happens in *The Edible Woman* except the wrong person gets married. And the person who embodies the restrictive forces in society is in fact the person Marian gets engaged to. In a standard comedy, he would be the defiant hero. As it is, he and the restrictive society are blended into one, and the comedy situation would be a tragic solution for Marian.[3]

To Sandler she added, again about *The Edible Woman*,

> In traditional comedy, boy meets girl, there are complications, the complications are resolved, and the couple is united. In my book the couple is not united, and the wrong couple gets married. The complications are resolved, but not in a way that reaffirms the social order.[4]

Yet the structural similarities observed above between *The Edible Woman*, *Surfacing*, and *Lady Oracle*—alienation followed by desperation, escape, and reintegration—are in their bare outline the actual structure of comedy, as in the Shakespearean sequence of social disorder, exile into the green world, reintegration, and return to 'natural' order.[5] I believe Atwood unintentionally misleads us when she uses the term "anti-comedy".[6] For while these three novels do not result in the healing of society, they do result in the healing of the individual—even minimally —to survive in that society. And while her green world is not the Forest of Arden or the Indian home of Congreve's Sir Oliver Surface, it is an equally valid one for twentieth-century writing

—the personal unconscious. The "right couple" may not get married, the social order may not be affirmed, but by the end of all three novels the principal character has achieved self-insight every bit as significant to the contemporary reader as Prospero's regaining of Milan and Miranda's marriage to Ferdinand were to Shakespeare's first audiences.

Atwood's denouements leave her narrators—like Shakespeare's Miranda—in a deeply-flawed world about which they still hold some illusions. *Lady Oracle*'s Joan Foster is, in fact, a parody-Miranda—naive, sentimental even as a mature woman, and at the end of the book seemingly on the verge of repeating her characteristic excessive-trust/excessive-mistrust cycle with yet another man. She surpasses Miranda in having fantasies of evil about the world as well as fantasies of the brave and new. Her story is her discovery of how she has projected Gothic malevolence and glamour onto ordinary people—of how she has made her tweedy husband into the Brontean lover she imagines at the heart of her fictional maze. She also discovers that this projection has prevented her from experiencing her friends and husband as real people, and from identifying the *actual* threats which some of them (often through their own fantasies) constitute to her. Yet at the end of the book, as she impulsively rushes off to treat as a helpless young man the journalist she so recently perceived as a hired killer, she is about to throw away this discovery and embark on a further illusion. The killer/nice young man dichotomy is, after all, the basic distortion in her image of the world—her view of her father as both possible murderer and a healing doctor, of the 'daffodil man' of her childhood as both molester and rescuer, of her husband Arthur as both "furtive" (*LO*, 4) and "idealistic" (*LO*, 165). Here and throughout the book she is portrayed by Atwood as a bright but limited person—naive in her insights into other people, shallow in her expectations of life, passive in doing little to direct the course of her life, and particularly limited in her literary tastes.

Marian MacAlpin is the closest to Miranda—the ingenue whose limitations are those of youth and who may grow through experience.

She is a willing initiate into the world of big business and bourgeois rationality, not because she believes in this world (as Joan Foster does) but because she has never been caused to disbelieve it. Her story is her discovery not of a personal fantasy of violence but of a very real, predatory, and entrapping violence in the external world. This is a stage beyond the discovery Joan makes and steps back from.

The narrator of *Surfacing* is yet a stage further. She is a cynic, having long ago realized that most of her fellow man have become as brutal and power-hungry as the machinery which a technological society serves, and has learned to protect herself with a mechanical kind of efficiency of her own. Her story is the discovery of the predatory and mechanical within herself— the discovery that in her 'adjustive' coping with the debased humanity around her (through abortion, repression, hypocrisy, etc.) she has become one of them.

Viewed this way, Joan, Marian, and the unnamed narrator of *Surfacing* appear as various incarnations of similar women. Joan struggles to clear away her delusions of romantic violence so she can see the actual world. Marian, in touch with the actual and by the end of the novel aware of its real violence, takes defensive measures which may eventually make her as much in need of reclamation as the narrator of *Surfacing*. And the latter has had a Marian MacAlpin breakdown in her past (a disillusioning affair with a married man) which has apparently made her the efficiently repressed person who greets us at the book's beginning. All together they reveal three stages of illusion—fantasy, convention, and cynicism—each concealing the routine pain and hurt of life.

•

"*I have to recant, give up the old belief that I'm powerless*..." decides *Surfacing*'s narrator on its final page. All three of Atwood's narrators are marked by extreme passivity. Marian feels fated to marry, and feels at the mercy of unconscious forces in agreeing to marry Peter, for whom she cares very little.

> Of course I'd always assumed through highschool and college that I was going to marry someone eventually and have children, everyone does.... But although I'm sure it was at the back of my mind I hadn't consciously expected it to happen so soon or quite the way it did. Of course I was more involved with Peter all along than I wanted to admit. (*EW*, 102)

In *Surfacing* the protagonist feels helpless to change her life or to alter the character of her relationship with her lover Joe. *Lady Oracle* brings such passivity into sharp focus. Joan essentially drifts from job to job, relationship to relationship. There is little that she passionately wants from life, and nothing that she has is she passionately attached to. She becomes Paul's mistress because "if you find yourself in a situation you can't get out of gracefully, you might as well pretend you chose it" (*LO*, 149). She meets her husband Arthur by "accident" (134), and agrees to marry him because she "couldn't think of any reasons why not" (197).

•

Lady Oracle is divided into five parts—Part I concerns Joan's exile in Italy; Part II her childhood in Toronto; Part III her young adulthood in England; Part IV her marriage to Arthur and escape through pretended suicide; Part V her resolution of her exile. This division reflects Atwood's gradual development of a psychoanalytic perspective throughout the three novels. In *Lady Oracle* she gives us a large view of Joan Foster's early life and makes it clear that most of Joan's difficulties with adult relationships are caused by transferences and projections from childhood experiences. A mother who is narcissistic and isolated, and a father who is absent, aloof, and through war duties and his work as an anaesthetist has had the power of life and death over others, together lock Joan into relationships with similarly aloof men to whom she metaphorically gives life and death power over herself. Consequently with both her lover Paul and her husband Arthur she relives her parents' drama of the unfulfilled, isolated, and dependent woman linked to an aloof and undemonstrative man.

In *The Edible Woman* Atwood provided no such psychological perspective. She gave Marian no childhood or adolescence; consequently the threats Marian perceives (and which she often chooses to live in the presence of) seem more actual than projected; her choices to live with them seem unmotivated, almost inevitable. For a perceptive reader, aware that these threats are not actual but are rather projections of Marian's inner life, her character has unsatisfyingly little depth. Why does she see her employer as a heartless parent, her fiancé Peter as a predator, his apartment building as a giant robotized organism? Why has she chosen Peter as her fiancé or Ainsley as her roommate? Why has she chosen Duncan as friend and part-time lover? Marian's own explanations that these seemed like practical and convenient choices do not answer our more fundamental questions of why Marian has so little passion for life, of why she has believed herself satisfied with the practical and the convenient.

The protagonist of *Surfacing* is a literary advance on Marian MacAlpin if only in possessing a fuller psychological life. Marian lives a consciousness unaware of its private motives and dramas; the protagonist of *Surfacing* is searching for these motives in memory, in artifact, and in her fantasies and unconscious associations. The opening page in which she rides back to her childhood home recollecting the family members of thirty years before announces this search. The family as a ground for the adult present is asserted six pages later in the image of the "father moose with a trench-coat and pipe in his mouth, a mother moose in a print dress and flowering hat and a little boy moose in short pants, a striped jersey and baseball cap, waving an American flag." Seen only after is the figure of the fourth member of the family, "a little girl moose in a frilly skirt and a pigtailed blonde wig, holding a red parasol in one hoof"—a figure which both completes the narrator's family and establishes her uneasy relationship with it.

Like Marian MacAlpin and Joan Foster, this woman has only superficial and awkward relationships with others. Her "best woman friend," she tells us, is someone she has known for "two months" (*S*, 10); in the arms of her lover Joe she feels detached, inanimate, and sees herself feeding "him unlimited supplies of nothing" (*S*, 84). The root of these limited relationships seems to lie in a mother whom she remembers mainly as an unemotional 'preserver,' a photographer who gathered "successive incarnations of me preserved and flattened like flowers pressed in dictionairies" (*S*, 69), and a father who preferred animals to people—"animals, he said, were more consistent, their behavior at least was predictable" (*S*, 59)—and presumably preferred animals to his own daughter. Certainly she is still in search of a father when she becomes the lover of her art teacher and finds in him someone equally uninterested in humanity as was her actual father.

> I worshipped him, non-child-bride, idolater, I kept the scraps of his writing like saints' relics, he never wrote letters, all I had was the criticism in red pencil he paperclipped to my drawings. C's and D's, he was an idealist, he said he didn't want our relationship as he called it to influence his aesthetic judgment. He didn't want our relationship to influence anything; it was to be kept separate from life. (*S*, 148-149)

When this relationship ends in a pragmatic abortion ("like getting a wart removed," *S*, 144), she is unable to talk about it to either parent because of their ignorance ("innocence") of life and of their daughter. "They never knew, about that or why I left. Their own innocence, the reason I couldn't tell them; perilous innocence, closing them in glass, their artificial garden, greenhouse," (*S*, 144).

•

> ...on the sodden trunks are colonies of plants, feeding on disintegration, laurel, sundew the insect eater, its toenail-sized leaves sticky with red hairs. Out of the leaf nests the flowers rise, pure white, flesh of gnats and midges, petals now, metamorphosis. (*S*, 167)

This image of the sundew, perceived by *Surfacing*'s narrator just as she begins her therapeutic descent into an 'insane' rejection of civilization and mankind, is the basic image of all three novels: a new order out of disorder; purity and integrity out of disintegration; personal wholeness out of mental collapse. Even more than embodying the structure of comedy, it embodies the structure of psychoanalytical therapy, of the descent into the neurosis to build a new life on the subject's own long-lost but intrinsically healthy roots. In psychoanalysis the subject goes down into his unconscious to explore his fantasies, rationalizations, illusions, the projections and transferences which have distorted his view of both himself and his world. So the narrator of *Surfacing* can eventually tell herself regarding her abortion,

> ...I couldn't accept it, that mutilation, ruin I'd made, I needed a different version, I'd pieced it together the best way I could, flattening it, scrapbook, collage, pasting over the wrong parts. A faked album, the memories fraudulent as passports.... (*S*, 143-144)

The process is reductive, destructive—in *Surfacing* beginning with the destruction of the false biography which the woman has unconsciously adopted for herself and later symbolized in her ritual destruction of dishes, books, and clothing in her parents' house. In *Lady Oracle* it involves Joan's recognition of her transferences from her "killer/healer" father to all the men of her life—the hero of the Costume-Gothic romances which she writes, her turtle-necked husband Arthur.

> *Cunningly he began his transformations.... His face grew a white gauze mask, then a pair of mauve-tinted spectacles, then a red beard and mustache, which faded, giving place to burning eyes and icicle teeth. Then his cloak vanished and he stood looking at her sadly; he was wearing a turtle-neck sweater....* (*LO*, 342)

This recognition is explicit, and vividly reductive. "No," she said. "I know who you are." "The flesh fell away from his face, revealing the skull behind it; he stepped towards her, reaching for her throat" (*LO*, 343).

As in the Freudian theory of catharsis, the exposure of the neurosis, the making of the unconscious force conscious, not only should cause it to lose its power, but should also make room for the long stifled elements of the authentic self to grow. This pattern of increasingly conscious neurosis, reduction and simplification of the neurotic actions, followed by tentative reconstruction is the pattern of all three novels. Marian MacAlpin's unconscious fear of being devoured 'surfaces' as an increasing aversion to food and culminates in a realization that "what she really wanted...had been reduced to simple safety" (*EW*, 263). The realization takes place in a snowy ravine which her friend Duncan describes as "close to absolute zero," "as near as possible to nothing." When she returns to her apartment and decides on her first positive action in days, to bake a woman-shaped cake for Peter, it is with a profound sense of personal new beginning.

> Her image was taking shape. Eggs. Flour. Lemons for the flavour. Sugar, icing-sugar, vanilla, salt, food-colouring. She wanted everything new, she didn't want to use anything that was already in the house. (*EW*, 267)

In *Surfacing* the narrator experiences a similar domination by 'surfacing' unconscious elements—fear of people, enclosures, clothing—which quickly reduces not only the food she can eat but all aspects of life. From the onset, however, she experiences also a promise of new life... "nothing has died, everyone's alive, everything is waiting to become alive" (*S*, 159). Her hallucinations bring her dreams and visions of her parents which appear to resolve her old dependences on them.

> Our father, Our Mother, I pray, Reach down for me, but it won't work: they dwindle, grow, become what they were, human. Something I never gave them credit for; ...
>
> I try to think for the first time what it was like to be them. (*S*, 189-190)

When her hallucinations end, she feels free to begin life again, particularly in her relationship to her previously uncommunicative lover Joe—"If I go with him we will have to talk, wooden houses are obsolete, and we can no longer live in spurious peace by avoiding each other, the way it was before, we will have to begin" (*S*, 192).

Of the three novels, *Lady Oracle* has the most convincing ending because there the narrator's commitment to renewal is tentative rather than total, and exists side-by-side with regressive fantasies. Joan's recognition of the unconscious patterns which have dominated her life occurs as she writes the final chapter of her last Gothic novel, *Stalked by Love*. Particularly clear to her is the pattern of passively waiting for the killer/ healer to take her away, "rescue" her, "a strong arm about her waist" (*LO*, 343). Clear also to her is her tendency to flee from any crisis like a Gothic heroine, "climbing out a window, in my bibbed apron and bun, oblivious to the cries of the children and grandchildren behind me. I might as well face it, I thought, I was an artist, an escape artist" (*LO*, 335). The new for Joan consists of not passively awaiting the next man to walk through her door, but clubbing this rather friendly newspaper reporter with a Cinzano bottle. It consists also of not running away from the consequences of this act—

> ...I could have escaped; he wouldn't have been able to trace me. I'm surprised I didn't do that since I've always been terrified of being found out. But somehow I couldn't just run off and leave him in the hospital with no one to talk to; not after I'd almost killed him by mistake. (*LO*, 344)

Yet this is not a thoroughly new Joan. Her speech is as naive and anxious as it is anywhere in the narrative; her act of assertion with the Cinzano bottle is a patently schizoid instance of transference. Her decision to stay with the reporter seems grounded not only in a new sense of self but in a new fantasy not too dissimilar from the organizing fantasy of the nurse novels of her first lover, Paul—"He's a nice man; he doesn't have a very interesting nose, but I have to admit that there is something about a man in a bandage..." (*LO*, 345). While Joan is making significant changes in her life, she does not seem ready to change it totally.

•

"Metamorphosis"—so the narrator of *Surfacing* described the growth of new "pure white" flowers of the sundew from the old flesh of gnats and midges, as she began to pursue her own transformation through destruction and simplification. To reach the sundew, she leaves her companions and paddles her canoe deep into a swamp, a "shore maze" (*S*, 167). In *Lady Oracle*, the metamorphosis of a caterpillar into a butterfly is the ruling metaphor, established both in Joan's failure as an overweight child to qualify as a 'butterfly' for a ballet recital (*LO*, 47) and in the spiritualist Mr. Smith's parable about the pessimistic and optimistic caterpillars (*LO*, 106). Metamorphosis becomes Joan's main hope; "I was hoping for magical transformations" (*LO*, 43) she tells us, as she yearns to dance like a butterfly or 'fly up' from Brownies to Girl Guides (*LO*, 52). Her attempts at transformation—from fat girl to thin woman, from high-school dropout to secret author of Costume Gothics and celebrity author of *Lady Oracle*, from housewife to mistress of the Royal Porcupine—remain partial and unsatisfying. Each new reality seems merely a trick or an illusion.

> When I looked at myself in the mirror, I didn't see what Arthur saw. The outline of my former body still surrounded me, like a mist, like a phantom moon, like the image of Dumbo the Flying Elephant superimposed on my own. (*LO*, 216)

Her final attempt to change—from an 'escape artist' to one who faces consequences, from a passive accepter of life to an active shaper of it—seems fuller and deeper because it is based not on acts of will which leave the unconscious life unchanged but on unconscious recognitions achieved through carthartic reductions or 'breakdown.' As in *Surfacing*, these occur in a maze (appropriately symbolic of the unconscious): the ancient garden maze of *Stalked by Love*'s Redmond Grange. As in *Surfacing* also, these recognitions are accompanied by yet another symbol of descent into the unconscious: the plunge into water (both Joan's mock suicide in Lake Ontario [LO 303] and Felicia's suicide and return from the dead in *Stalked by Love* [*LO*, 322-333]) from within which a new and more authentic self can emerge.

•

Before this point in *Lady Oracle*, before Joan's reaching of some true metamorphosis by 'plunging' into the 'maze' of the unconscious, she has experienced reality as duplicitous, ambiguous, constantly undergoing metamorphoses of its own. These metamorphoses, like her own from fat girl to thin woman, are false ones also. Out of touch, for example, with her unconscious view of men as simultaneously killers and rescuers like her father, she is plagued by her projection of this view onto the basically unremarkable men she leads her life with. These illusory metamorphoses appear to be resolvable for her when she herself changes.

> Every man I'd ever been involved with, I realized, had had two selves: my father healer and killer; the man in the tweed coat, my rescuer and possibly also a pervert; the Royal Porcupine and his double, Chuck Brewer; even Paul, whom I'd always believed had a sinister other life I couldn't penetrate. (*LO*, 295)

This illusory doubleness is a characteristic given to men by the narrators of the other novels also. Marian sees Peter as both an "impressive" young lawyer and as a sadistic hunter with "a snarl of teeth" (*EW*, 244). The woman of *Surfacing* can both "worship" her first lover and believe him a murderer. For her, a new beginning also means a resolution of this doubleness: "He was neither of the things I believed, he was only a normal man, middle-aged, second-rate, selfish and kind in the average proportions..." (*S*, 189).

•

All three of Atwood's novels are comic novels, that is, optimistic of human reconciliation and renewal. While their structure in some sense resembles the traditional comic one of order, retreat to the green world, and re-establishment of order (often symbolized in marriage or birth), it is closer to contemporary models such as the psychoanalytic one of neurosis, catharsis, and self-actualization or literary ones such as deconstruction and invention. Certainly there is something specifically contemporary in these books, something that speaks to its own time in a more meaningful way than the mere *issues* of women's liberation, ecological preservation, or literary nationalism—all of which are invoked by the books and occasionally have been used to explain them. There is something contemporary also about their protagonists who are concerned almost totally with personal salvation; like the protagonists of Heller, Kroetsch, Hawkes, or Barthelme, they imply by their actions that the world can be saved only by each individual taking responsibility for saving himself.

The preoccupation of the novels is with overcoming passivity and transference so as to perceive the present clearly and engage with it. The difficulty which the protagonists encounter in engaging with the present links them firmly to the fearful and detached voice of Atwood's poetry. Atwood's attempt in the novels to resolve this fear implies a critique of the woman of her poetry, invites her to struggle toward a wider ground for relationship than irony and distrust.

In the fiction, wider ground challenges technique. In both the second and third novels there is an increase in narrative complexity over the previous one. The first-person narrative in *The Edible Woman* follows one chronology with a significant shift to the third person during Marian's breakdown. The narrative of *Surfacing* indicates three time periods (Marian's childhood, years at artschool, and the present) and makes use of the unreliability of a first-person narrator to provide two levels of reality—the "lies" the narrator has told herself about her experiences and the actual events these lies conceal. The technique of the narrative is to blend these elements into the conventional consciousness flow of psychological realism. *Lady Oracle*'s narrative includes four time periods, and two levels of reality— Joan's conscious beliefs about event and her more perceptive unconscious beliefs that are manifested in her gothic fantasies. The technique combines stream of consciousness with collaged chunks of the narrator's Costume Gothics. Since both the narrator and the reader soon learn that the latter contain insights into the anxieties of the former, the overall effect is that of the detective novel in which the crime is known but the resolution, and the way to this resolution, are not.

•

"You Are Here" a cryptic sign informed the narrator of Atwood's early poem "A Night in the Royal Ontario Museum." "Where is here?" Atwood herself asked rhetorically in *Survival,* saying "It is what a man asks when he finds himself in unknown territory" (17). For the women of Atwood's novels and poems, their own lives are "unknown territory." "If the man is really lost," Atwood continued in *Survival,* "he may also wonder how he got 'here' to begin with" and "take stock of what 'here' really contains." These are the solutions of the narrators of *Surfacing* and *Lady Oracle* and the unconsciously reached solutions of the more limited Marian MacAlpin. Each time 'here' is a better place than we, or they, believed.

---

1. References are to *The Edible Woman* (Toronto: McClelland & Stewart, 1969), hereafter *EW*; *Surfacing* (Toronto: McClelland & Stewart, 1972), hereafter *S*; and *Lady Oracle* (Toronto: McClelland & Stewart, 1976); hereafter *LO*.

2. "Atwood Walking Backwards," *Open Letter*, Second Series, No. 5 (Summer 1973), 75-76.

3. In Graeme Gibson, *Eleven Canadian Novelists* (Toronto: House of Anansi, 1973), p. 21.

4. *The Malahat Review*, 41, January 1977, p. 13.

5. Atwood's sequence could be described as personal disorder, exile into the individual unconscious, reintegration, and a 'surfacing' to increased personal wholeness.

6. An instance of such being misled is Sherrill Grace's unquestioning and largely borrowed statement that *The Edible Woman* "is a witty, sarcastic, urbane anti-comedy which does not offer the traditional comic reaffirmation of the social order" (*Violent Duality: a Study of Margaret Atwood*, Montreal: Vehicule Press, 1980, p. 87).

SEXUAL IMAGERY IN SINCLAIR ROSS

> It was Jenny's first circus. A girl in purple tights, erect on a galloping horse, a red coated brass band, a clown, an elephant ripped through the middle. 'And did you see the elephant?' she asked her brother Tom, who had found the piece of poster in the street when he was in the town marketing the butter and eggs.
>
> ("Circus in Town," *The Lamp at Noon*, 68[1])

Throughout the stories of Sinclair Ross' *The Lamp at Noon*, animals, both exotic and domestic, carry news of the imagination—of beauty, vitality, even sexual excitement—to rural characters such as the eleven-year-old Jenny. Often the images of these animals are limited and flawed, like the "elephant ripped through the middle." Often they are impossibly stereotyped and romanticized, like the incandescent sexual images here, the "purple tights," the "red coated brass band." Yet for many of the characters they offer a psychologically real alternative to the routines, the "marketing" of "butter and eggs," that paralyze their emotional lives.

Linked to these animals are art and music, not the music taught to farm boys by teachers who "count right through" to a metronome, but music that says "that life was worth living," that comes "flashing gallant through the night."

> ...the notes were piercing, golden as the cornet itself, and they gave life expanse that it had never never known before. They floated up against the night, and each for a moment hung there clear and visible. Sometimes they mounted poignant and sheer. Sometimes they soared and then, like a bird alighting, fell and brushed earth again.
>
> ("Cornet at Night," *LN*, 49)

Contrasted to the music and animals are both conventional concepts of culture—here "the parlour with its genteel plushiness," a mother's hopes that her son will "behave like a Christian and a gentleman" (*LN*, 37)—and the practical considerations of farm life. In this story the music causes a "sleepy old plow horse" (*LN*,40) to gallop off with the farm wagon across the prairie, spilling the family groceries into ditches and badger holes. The cornet-player's hands are unable to learn to stook wheat and he is sent away by adults too preoccupied with field and parlour to understand what their son has learned from him—"a harvest, however lean, is certain each year, but a cornet at night is golden only once" (*LN*, 51).

•

The adult characters in Ross' stories have usually had their awareness of nature, beauty, and their own emotional lives deadened by the struggle to subsist on stony farms frequently stricken by drought and hail. Yet while these characters have lost the power of emotional communication with their spouses and children, they often remain open to the emotional call of animals. In "The Runaway" a careful middle-aged farmer trades four steers for two "superb" black Diamond mares of which he has "no real need" and which his wife derides as "a team of fancy horses."

> The next day, however, she changed her mind. She even primped and curled a little, and found a bright ribbon for her hat. My father too, made his preparations. He washed the democrat, greased the axels, carefully cleaned and polished his two best sets of harness, and finally, after dinner, changed into his Sunday suit and a clean white shirt. (*LN*, 86)

It is as though the black horses have magically returned them to a time of physical awareness, courtship, and vitality.

> ...as the Diamonds plunged away there was such a girlish peal of laughter from my mother! They were young again. My father had a team of Diamonds, and my mother had something that his enormous passion for them had taken from her twenty years ago. Walking over the potato patch I realized that they couldn't possibly have taken me with them. Today's events, properly understood, were all before my time. (*LN*, 86)

•

Often, as in the previous two stories, the narrator is a young boy whose own emerging masculinity rests precariously on the energies of these animals and on his hopes for a reawakening of similar energies in his father. (A variant of this is the story "One's a Heifer" in which the boy-narrator has only an uncle "laid up for the winter with sciatica." The absent father is replaced by the mad farmer Arthur Vickers, who further confuses the boy's sexual vision by appearing to have murdered a young woman and hidden her body in a box stall. Through the stall, passion is again linked with the animal world, although here twisted by repression and solitude.) Thus the narrator of "The Runaways" openly hopes, when the Diamonds are offered in trade, that his father "will be weak and take them" ("weak," that is, in practical terms, but strong in terms of passion). In "Cornet at Night" the narrator finds in the cornet-player an alternative father who can help him bring to the piano-music his mother obliges him to study a passion long forgotten by his father. In "The Outlaw," the boy discovers that his daring, against his parents' orders, to ride the family's untamed man-killing mare brings out an unsuspected "pride" in both his father and his mother, as if they had been unconsciously wanting to live out their romantic fantasies through him. "How long," the boy wonders, "had I kept them waiting? How many times in the last few months had they looked at me and despaired?" In this discovery the boy senses that his sexuality has at last been confirmed, and that he is free both to ride the forbidden horse Isabel and to pursue his grade-school girlfriend. "...in their peculiar parental idiom, they had just given their permission, and Isabel and the future were all mine. Isabel and Millie Dickson" (*LN*, 34).

•

Indeed it is a "peculiar parental idiom" in which forbidding can become hoping and concern become permission. But adults in Ross' stories frequently convey ambiguous or contradictory messages, especially when animals enter their relationships. In "The Lamp at Noon" Paul feels moved to embrace his fearful wife, but "responding to a kind of instinct that he must withstand her, that it was his self-respect and manhood against the fretful weakness of a woman" (*LN*, 18), holds himself still. Yet moments later in the barn he feels no restraint about embracing his bay mare—"they stood a long time, motionless, comforting and assuring each other" (*LN*, 19). Similarly, John in "A Field of Wheat" presents a calm face to his wife after their crop is devastated by hail, yet in his barn falls sobbing "against one of the horses, his head pushed into the big deep hollow of its neck and shoulders, one hand hooked by the fingers in the mane, his own shoulders drawn up and shaking" (*LN*, 81). For these men emotions seem to be repressed from people, but released toward animals. For them it is the animal rather than the human that can be trusted to respond to emotion or imagination. Will, in "Not by Rain Alone," is "on edge" talking to his wife, finds it "exasperation to have to start telling her about the muddy roads," is unable to transcend his anxiety about the farm to reach out to her. But when he looks at his mare Bess, he can be moved to observe possibilities he would never be free to find in a woman.

> Bess had imagination. Every day for three uncurbed minutes she was really free; and despite her wariness, despite the heavy harness clanking at her sides, she plunged across the yard to savour and exploit them. Neck arching a moment, slim body rearing in illusion of release. She dashed a hundred yards along the road; another plunge and whirl, then back spent and depressed, to let him lead her to her stall. (*LN*, 54)

For him, this mare becomes an image of his history and needs with woman, the responsive woman he has wanted but never had. Its belly "starting to sag a little," its "angular" hip bones recall for him his mother "wizened" also by farm work, "with tight grim lip and work-thin, stubborn hands." Its "dainty startled prick-up of the ears" and "imperious" mannerisms remind him of the liveliness he rightly feared his fiancee would lose through farm work if he married her.

•

Repeatedly in Ross' stories one finds that the channels of emotional communication between humans have been blocked —by convention, fear, loneliness—and that only animals can lead them to expressions of strong feeling. Sexual feelings are almost impossible to these characters, except through the symbolism of animals. The boy-narrators experience their parents as having no sexual life, as having responses circumscribed by the demands of farm and church. For the narrator of "The Outlaw," the man-killing horse Isabel is, as its name hints, a Jezebel, a temptress, a *femme fatale*.

> She was beautiful but dangerous. She had thrown one man and killed him, thrown another and broken his collarbone, and my

> parents...never let a day go by without giving lurid details, everything from splints and stitches to the undertaker, of the painful and untimely end in store for me should I ever take it into my fool young head to ride her. (*LN*, 24)

At first he does not see how his parents have sublimated their own needs for excitement into the horse, how their "lurid" accounts represent their own repressed excitements and imaginings, not see how the outlaw horse locked in its stall is the family's own locked-up passions—"a captive, pining her heart away" (*LN*, 24). Nor does he see how his own vision of the mare ("To approach her was to be enlarged, transported. She was coal-black, gleaming, queenly. Her mane had a ripple and her neck an arch. And somehow, softly and mysteriously, she was always burning. The reflection on her glossy hide, whether of winter sunshine or yellow lantern light, seemed to glow of some fierce, secret passion. There were moments when I felt the whole stable charged with her, as if she were the priestess of her kind, in communion with her diety [sic]." [*LN*,24]) is a direct reflection of the parents' belief that sexuality and overt emotion are exotic, unnatural, and dangerous. Only at the end does he glimpse the parents' subjective involvement in the horse, the vicarious pleasure his father, in particular, takes in his son's having ridden her. Here the father's question is not about the boy's safety, but rather the familiar locker-room question between men. "'But the mare,' my father interrupted in a man-to-man tone of voice, abruptly cold-shouldering my mother, 'how did you find her?'" (*LN*, 33)

•

Despite the boy's exhilaration at being allowed to pursue his passions for both horses and women, his having to carry his father's sexuality in this pursuit is a significant price to pay for such freedom. The children in Ross' stories do pay for their parents' repressions—in "The Lamp at Noon" one pays with a life, in "Not by Bread Alone" another pays with his wife's life, in "A Field of Wheat" two seem about to pay with their emotional lives. The point-of-view character in this latter story is Martha, their mother; again her sexual feelings are sublimated, but into a wheat field rather than an animal.

> It was the best crop of wheat that John had ever grown, sturdy, higher than the knee, the heads long and filling well; ...she stopped, holding her apron with one hand and with the other stroking the blades of grain that pressed close to her skirts, luxuriant and tall. (*LN*, 73)

The phallic overtones of this passage are reinforced by her reflections that follow on her husband's ten-year struggle to grow what has deprived her of his "love," of his "deep strong laughter that used to make her feel she was living at the heart of things." They are reinforced also by her sudden sense here of a "freshening promise" that "she and John—mightn't there be a little of life left for them too? A man was young at thirty-nine. And if she didn't have to work so hard, if she could get some new clothes, maybe some of the creams and things that other women had...." (*LN*, 75) The concluding ellipsis is hers, and seems itself to point to new stirrings.

The animal symbol for unrepressed sexuality in this story is the family dog. It bounds into the story with Martha's son Joe and daughter Isabel, playing exuberantly with the younger boy while the girl berates him with her mother's characteristic bitterness.

> 'Do you know what Joe's done? He's taken off all his clothes and he's in the trough with Nipper.' She was a lanky girl...but spoiled by an expression that strained her mouth and brows into a reproachful primness. It was Martha who had taught her the expression,.... (*LN*, 75)

The girl's acquired prudishness expresses itself in the expected animal images. "You're just a dirty little pig anyway," she tells her brother. "And the horses don't want to drink after you've been in the trough."

The boy and dog seem almost indistinguishable in their irrepressibility. "Joe squealed, and excited by the scuffle, Nipper yelped and splattered Martha with a spray of water from his coat and tail" (*LN*, 76).

After the hailstorm destroys the crop and damages the house, the family finds Nipper "beaten lifeless" at the front door. In the wheat field are only "here and there an isolated straw standing bolt upright in headless defiance." And while the story continues to detail Martha's despair and her husband's humiliation, the sexual potential of their lives is already clear.

•

> We've lost El Greco. Driven by hunger the coyotes lately have been coming right to the outskirts of the town, and about eleven o'clock last night when they started howling again he answered with such a furious barking that I got frightened and opened the door for him. Philip ran after him, and stayed out so long trying to whistle him back that he froze his ears. There was no more howling from the coyotes, though, so we've concluded that they lured him well away from town, then turned and made an end of him. (*AMMH*, 149)

This is Mrs. Bentley's curious summary of another animal's fate in Ross' best-known novel, *As For Me and My House*. It occurs late in the book after her reliability as a narrator has been undermined by her patronizing of her husband's physical skills (*AMMH*, 1-2, 63, 133-134), by her naive belief that her initial and rather calculated interest in him (16) was a sufficient basis for a sexual relationship, by her blaming the failure of their subsequent marriage on cramped houses, small hypocritical towns, and the prairie wind, and by her tendency to cliché self-rationalizations. "It's a woman's way, I suppose, to keep on trying to subdue a man, to bind him to her, and it's a man's way to keep on just as determined to be free" (*AMMH*, 64). Mrs. Bentley's conviction that El Greco has met his death with the coyotes parallels such rationalizations about the roles of men and women—men as "wolfhounds," restless and death-seeking, and women as homebuilders, afraid and unadventurous. Her unmarried friend Paul takes the male side of this view when he tells her "that in a hound's life bread and milk and safety can never make up for the excitement of a single kill" (*AMMH*, 149). The polarization of safety and danger are the same as in her earlier analysis of her husband.

> I've comforted myself... trying to be a good wife, seeing religiously that his socks were always darned, his books in order, his dinner hot. But it was all wrong. Comfort and routine were the last things he needed. Instead he ought to have been out mingling with his own kind.... He ought to have had the opportunity to live, to be reckless, spendthrift, bawdy, anything but what he is, what I've made him. (*AAMH*, 103)

From what we know of Mrs. Bentley's own hesitancies around passion— her abrupt giving up of a musical career in order to acquire Philip as her husband, her feigning sleep when Philip comes to bed— this polarization strikes us as a projection. There must be other possibilities—even for El Greco—than the alternative ones of emotional paralysis or spendthrift death.

•

Yet in two of Ross' later novels Mrs. Bentley's dichotomous view of sexuality as a force which destroys unless repressed, is openly the view of the author. In both *The Well* (1958) and *Whir of Gold* (1970) the horses of various stories of *The Lamp at Noon* return, but in transfigured contexts. Minnie, the young boy Chris' horse in *The Well*, is "smart and mean and pretty" like Isabel of "The Outlaw," and like the boy of that story, Chris makes his father "proud" by having the "nerve" to ride her. However, Minnie throws Chris many times, and eventually, frightened by a slipping saddle, tramples him to death. In reaction, the father irrationally shoots the horse, and pays the beautiful but mean-spirited Sylvia $2000 a year to marry him. Both actions repudiate the life of excitement and mystery. In *Whir of Gold* the actual Isabel and her boy rider return. The horse again stands "in a halo of outlaw lightning... dramatic, radiant" in contrast to the boy's "work-bent, blindly practical father."

> She was coal-black, gleaming, queenly. Her mane had a ripple and her neck an arch. And somehow, softly and mysteriously, she was always burning.... There were moments when you felt the whole stable charged with her, as if she were the priestess of her kind, in communion with her deity. (*WG*, 52)

Yet in this novel, unlike the earlier story, the horse is not the gateway to emotional fulfillment but the first step to despair. Sonny's successful riding of Isabel, in defiance of his parents, leads him to experience actual sex as mundane; "I had taken her wanting revelation and had got instead a scratchy half-hour in the hay" (*WG*, 22). It leads him also to believe that such splendid, transcendent experiences as his riding of Isabel are impossible to a moral person because they are attainable only through transgression. While in "The Outlaw" Ross presented the ride as a life-affirmative rebellion, here he parallels it to Sonny's participation, as a young man, in a jewelry-store robbery. He has him reason that "Isabel would approve" of the robbery—

> just as she had approved when I took the law into my own hands, heedless of warnings, and saddled and rode her. For that matter, once I had done it, hadn't they approved too? After you've done what you want to do and got away with it, don't they always approve? (*WG*, 127)

Ross' message now is that Sonny's passions have all been tied by his parents to the impossibly romantic figure of Isabel. His father's investing of Isabel with "lurid" fantasy, and his subliminal message to his son that only disobedience can attain the transcendent experience, has left Sonny with the psychopathic conviction that the only fulfilling acts are illegal ones, and that these become legal by the very act of one's doing them. Ordinary, unforbidden pleasures—sex with a girlfriend, even performing jazz music which in the story "Cornet by Night" said that "life is worth living"—have become mundane, anti-climactic, in the light of that first defiant ride on Isabel. To live out his father's fantasies—i.e., 'taking the law into his own hands'—has become for Sonny more interesting than living his own life.

In addition, the horses in both *The Well* and *As For Me and My House* are associated by Ross with impulses of male exhibitionism that exclude women rather than move toward them. In *As for Me and My House* this association is given little emphasis, although it is clear neither Paul's horse Harlequin nor Steve's Minnie inspire the passions aroused by the horses of Ross' stories. Here they neither substitute for women nor awaken men toward women, but arouse only masculine bravado. Paul shows off his philological expertise throughout the book, and on horseback presents "a certain histrionic dash ... rigged out in all his cowboy togs, leather chaps, a bright red spotted handkerchief" (*AMMH*, 40). When the Bentleys agree to buy Steve a horse, he seems to Mrs. Bentley to have "a chilling way of taking everything as if it were his due. His only elation seems to be at the prospect of showing off in front of Horizon ..." (104). We can see in these images that both Paul and Steve are preoccupied with self-love; in Paul's case this narcissism seems to take precedence over any attraction he feels to Mrs. Bentley.

In *The Well* the impulse toward male exhibitionism contrasts to the feelings of intimacy and trust Chris Rowe experiences with horses. His first horseback ride makes him feel "indiscriminate in his need for someone to see him and be amazed." "What use could it be without someone to know him and be envious?" he thinks (45). He fantasizes himself wearing "silver-studded chaps, dark blue shirt, and scarlet bandanna," riding "a hot-eyed jet black stallion that no one else had ever dared to ride. Fierce, untamed—to mount him was to provide a spectacle of outlaw fury and consummate horsemanship" (52). This fantasy is connected to his feelings of "condescension" and "wily arrogance" (142) when he enters the town dancehall, and his sense of "amusement" and "mastery" (148) when he seduces the young girl Elsie Grover—as if she is (the phrase is the same as the one Ross employs for Steve's view of his horse) "his due" (149).

•

The chief similarity between the animals of *The Lamp at Noon* and those of the novels lies in Ross' use of them for characterization. Like the farmer-fathers of "The Outlaw" and "The Runaway," characters who like animals are cast as still alive to imagination. Chris Rowe of *The Well*, despite his background in petty crime and preoccupation with "bravado" (135), is made to appear redeemable by his affection for Norris the farm collie and by his easy rapport with the stallion North. Larson's cynicism toward the collie, together with his alternating anger and sentimentality toward the horse that killed his son, reflect a bitterness which has limited his life since the son's death. His wife Sylvia's refusal to milk cows or to let him keep pigs is used by Ross to mark her quickly as cold, potentially evil. In *Sawbones Memorial*, which contains very little nature imagery, the sympathetic central character Doc Hunter is nevertheless characterized by both positive sexual attitudes and affection for his "good horses."

•

Does El Greco in *As For Me and My House* die? Given Ross' equation throughout his writing of animals with passion and sex, given his linking of the dog, through his name, to Philip as artist, given his linking him with the "long and lean" figures of passionate life painted by the historical El Greco (81), and his opposing him to the genteel painters Romney and Gainsborough (105), this is a key question for any interpretation of the novel. His death is theoretically possible; the coyotes are "driven by hunger," Mrs. Bentley tells us, and cease howling shortly after he joins them. But may his death not be a projection by Mrs. Bentley of her own fears? We note that she also perceives El Greco to be sexually attracted to the coyotes.

> El Greco . . . broke into a long hollow bay that sounded less like defiance than response. All the way home the darkness was alive and slinking . . . All I could see were his wolfish eyes. (133-134)

We note further that the "wilderness" of prairie and coyote has for Mrs. Bentley throughout the novel often been synonymous with danger and masculine sexuality. "I wish I could reach him," she writes of her husband, "but it's like the wilderness outside of night and sky and prairie, . . ." (25). And we note further how pointedly Paul has encouraged her to see El Greco as a metaphor for Philip, his artistic passion bottled up inside his study, and his sexual energies unengaged by his marriage.

> "It really isn't right, such a fine dog going to waste, playing in the street and making a fool of himself. . . . He's ashamed inside: knows this isn't where he ought to be." (*AMMH*, 137)

When El Greco runs momentarily toward the prairie he remarks with a "disdain" that seems aimed at both the dog and Philip, "He's stopped now at the edge of town, afraid to go any farther. You don't need to worry. He'll be back for his blankets and bread and milk" (*AMMH*, 137).

•

The ambiguity surrounding the fate of El Greco stands almost a middle ground between Ross's treatment of sexual imagery in the stories of *The Lamp at Noon* and that in the later novels. The animals of the stories, all but one of which was written between 1934 and 1952, affirm the imaginative life as something at least within human memory; in many of the stories they encompass the family's sexual life; in "A Field of Wheat" the fate of the dog is the family's sexual fate. The animals of the novels from 1958 to 1974, however, can kill, as in *The Well*, can emotionally maim, as in *Whir of Gold*, or as in *Sawbones Memorial* have simply become irrelevant to human imagination. In the latter novel, while sexual affirmativeness still distinguishes the sympathetic characters from the unsympathetic, there is a notable lack of passion around both animals and sexuality, and no suggestion that sexual passion has energized even Doc Hunter's everyday work. Clearly some profound change occurs in Sinclair Ross' vision between the early stories and the later novels; Mrs. Bentley's fear for El Greco grows into the actual death of Chris Larson, and the limited lives of Sonny McAlpine and Doc Hunter.

•

It is the risks attendant on passion that have grown. In "The Runaway," the two black Diamond mares "brought a spark of wonder to the dullest eye" and reawoke energy and youth in the narrator's mother and father. They linked the father to the risks of reaching beyond the "ordinary" pleasures of El Greco's blankets and milk.

> ...a horseman more passionate and discerning than my father never lived. In ordinary circumstances, being genuine, he would probably have found satisfaction in ordinary horses, like the ones he owned— humble, worthy creatures, the only fault a lack of grace and fire—but there was a splendour about the Diamonds, a poise, a dramatic loftiness, that left in its wake a blight of shabbiness and discontent. Arching their necks like emperor horses, flinging their heads up, pealing trumpet neighs—how could my father *help* wanting them? (*LN*, 90).

This is the "splendour" that Philip Bentley dreams of, and that El Greco rushes to the coyotes to regain. It is the splendour also that Paul, Steve, and Chris Rowe in *The Well* can so easily convert to self-admiration. In "The Runaway," such splendour is unknown to the calculating Luke Taylor, who owns "a bathroom with hot and cold running water" (cf. the Larson bathroom in *The Well*) and "a mechanical piano that you played with pedals instead of your fingers," who "up and down the countryside" was "notorious for his shady deals" (84), and who sells the father the defective Diamonds. But even for unimaginative Luke Taylor the risks loom. There are risks in dealing in such creatures of "sun-sparked loveliness"; these descend on him when the team he has sold, spurred on with fire at his suggestion, gallop in terror with a flaming wagon-load back into his barnyard, delivering a spark of wonder indeed to his world of shady deals and foreclosed mortgages. The spark brings destruction of his barn, destruction of his twenty Black Diamonds, and his own death. We see that the spark of high-strung temperament proves an ambiguous blessing to his horses when they refuse in "fire-crazed resistance" to be led to safety.

It is the implications of this small incident—being burned by the fires of passion—which come to dominate Sinclair Ross's vision in the later novels and to doom much more attractive characters than Luke Taylor. In *Whir of Gold*, Sonny's passion for Isabel ruins his attraction to Millie Dickson and his life with Madeleine; in *The Well*, Chris Larson's passion for the horse Minnie kills him; Chris Rowe's passion for the scheming Sylvia implicates him in the murder of his benefactor; in *Sawbones Memorial*, sexual passion leads to child abuse, abortion, and suicide. In *As For Me and My House*, this bleak view expresses itself in the death by childbirth of Judith West—certainly a heavy price for one sexual adventure. This view is tempered, however, by the child which she bears to the Bentleys, and by the uncertainty of El Greco's fate. Perhaps, emulating Philip Bentley's fathering of Judith's child, El Greco lives on with a harem of coyotes, as the father in "The Runaway" lived on to breed more Black Diamonds, or the original boy of "The Outlaw" survived riding Isabel to ride on toward Millie Dickson.

---

1. This and subsequent references are to *The Lamp at Noon* (Toronto: McClelland & Stewart, 1968), hereafter *LN*; *As For Me and My House* (Toronto: McClelland & Stewart, 1957), hereafter *AMMH*; *The Well* (Toronto: Macmillan, 1958), hereafter *W*; *Whir of Gold* (Toronto: McClelland & Stewart, 1970), hereafter *WG*; and *Sawbones Memorial* (Toronto: McClelland & Stewart, 1978), hereafter *SM*.

THE LANGUAGE OF THE CONTEMPORARY CANADIAN LONG POEM

The first sign we see in the long poem is its length, promising to the reader that its matter is large in depth or breadth. Its length also speaks about time—that the writer will take his time, engage time, encompass its passage. Unlike the collection of 'occasional' poems, it says that time is not a series of discrete and unique occasions, but is large, can be viewed as large, can be apprehended, measured and entered, that there is time—time at least to read a long poem. There is even in the length of the long poem an announcement of futurity—in the commitment of the poet to enter a continuing structure (as Louis Dudek's current long poem *Continuation*, "an infinite poem in progress"), in the exemplary motion of line following line, page following page, section opening into section.

•

At one time the long poem was a story, a folk epic, an epic, an elegy, a romance; in Classical Rome and seventeenth and eighteenth-century

England it was also satire, didactic essay; later in Wordsworth and Whitman it became the story of an inner life, the story, increasingly episodic, of perception and reflection, becoming even more inward and episodic with Tennyson's *In Memoriam*; in our century the discursive or narrative line broke apart into the collaged segments of *The Waste Land*, the assembled documents, images, and contentions of *The Cantos*, the recollections regrouped on musical structure of Bunting's *Briggflatts*. In recent years narrative makes a comeback as the narrative of composition—the poem's subject becomes largely its own writing: Williams' *Paterson*, Olson's *Maximus Poems*, Dudek's *Europe*, Duncan's *Structure of Rime*, Bowering's *Genève*.

As someone engaged in writing long poems, and in reading both published and unpublished long poems, I see narrative as still the central issue of the form. Sequential narrative is an organizational system, a language, a structure of signs that speaks of certain assumptions about reality: that it is linear, directed by cause and effect, excluding in its constructions and focusses. In distrust of such assumptions writers have attempted to replace narrative as the long poem's dominant sign. Place has been substituted for sequential narrative in recent Canadian long poems to such an extent that it promises to become as much a convention as what it replaced: Everson's *Montreal*, Suknaski's *Wood Mountain Poems* and *In the Name of Narid*, Marshall's *West Coast Trail Poems*, McKay's *Long Sault*, Geddes' *Rivers Inlet*, Bowering's *Rocky Mountain Foot*, Marlatt's *Steveston*. In other long poems language itself—rhythm, syntax, word-play—has been given narrative's once dominant role—Nichol's *Martyrology*, Kroetsch's *The Sad Phoenician*, McCaffery's *Dr. Sadhu's Muffins*. In some, the recurrent image—Marlatt's rings, Blaser's moths, the sea of Dudek's *Atlantis*, the naked imagery and language of Webb's *Naked Poems*—provides the cohesion and focus once provided by plot. In still others, inventiveness, linguistic and narrative adventure, game, jest, and play have been made the dominant structure—notably Coleman's *Some Plays: on Words*, Nichol's *The True Eventual Story of Billy the Kid*, Kroetsch's *Seed Catalogue*.

•

"Over the edge of the dyke a river pours, uncalled for, unending," Marlatt writes in *Steveston*. Even in a poem of place, time pours, a narrative moves. The very structures writers have used to replace sequential narrative—collage, symphonic form, geography, play, recurrent image—become, if successful, other kinds of narrative, sources of motion, energy, and surprise. The poem ultimately becomes a narrative of this energy, the energy of a structure going through recognition, recurrence, and connection. In part, the length of the long poem derives from the wish of the writer to follow this energy as far as possible, with such results as Barbour's *Poem as Long as a Highway*, Dudek's *Continuation*, or Kroetsch's *Field Notes*, a "life-long poem." Kroetsch argues in a current issue of *Dandelion* that this impulse to prolong is a wish to delay; in this argument he reads the energy of the long poem as sexual energy, and delay as post-ponement of a terminating orgasm. This theory, in my subjective view, has unhappy implications for the life-long poem (not to mention the life itself should it bear any close relationship to the poem), and contains at least a hint of exclusively male perspective; not surprisingly, it is linked by Kroetsch to a view of the Canadian long poem as a narrative of disappointment and failure. I simply don't see the long poem this way; for me, in Kroetsch's metaphor, it requires recurring orgasm, movement from surprise to surprise, is prolonged not only to delay but to continue, it anticipates more rather than postpones the most. Individual sections of the poem can culminate, come briefly to rest, as well as lead into new moments in the larger work. This is how I read *Allophanes*, Kroetsch's own *Seed Catalogue*, Dudek's *Atlantis*—as moving in the joy of continuing and varied culmination rather than in a fear of ending.

•

It was Eliot in *The Waste Land* and *Four Quartets* who worked most deliberately against ending, by working not only against narrative but against the very movement of time. Paradoxically, two of his main techniques in *The Waste Land*, collage and the juxtaposition of text and subtext, are very much alive today in Canada as parts of the language of the time-affirming long poem. Collage suspends sequential narrative, works to contain time within a spatial structure. The juxtaposition of text with a subtext invites the comparison of past and present. Contemporary long poems have created new narrative structures by combining these systems, like Ondaatje's *The Collected Works of Billy the Kid* which is both a sequence of Billy's life and a collage of his 'collected works,' or Ken Norris' *Report on the Second Half of the Twentieth Century* which is both autobiography and a collage of life with newspaper document, or Marlatt's *Steveston* which collages perspectives of Steveston, relates its history, and plays its narratives against the subtext of the Kwakiutl Winter Ceremonial. Here collage is used not to freeze time but to imply sequences through juxtaposed blocks of image and incident. Yet the result is not linear sequence—the incidents tend to interrelate rather than to fall into linear pattern; the structures thus argue against linear causation, to propose some network of operative force.

•

Early examples of the use of subtext, such as Joyce's use of the Odyssey or Eliot's of the grail romances in *The Waste Land*, tended to involve subjects of high cultural standing; tended to create texts modelled on the structure of the subtext, tended to affirm some value in the subtext by casting the main text in an ironic relationship to it. The contemporary poem tends to use a subtext of low cultural standing, to do no borrowing of structure from it, and rarely to use it to subject the main text to ironic commentary. Contemporary subtexts include Bowering's use of the structure of baseball, Kroetsch's use of his ledger and seed catalogue, Atwood's use of Susanna Moodie's journals, the saga of Mrs. Fraser in Ondaatje's *The Man with Seven Toes*. I used Pratt's poem *The Titanic* in *The Clallam*, and the grail romances in my *King of Swords*, Bowering uses an entire potpourri of literary works in

Allophanes. In *King of Swords* and *Allophanes*, and also in Atwood's *Moodie*, any irony falls on the subtext rather than on the text; in the Kroetsch *Seed Catalogue*, the subtext openly replaces such items as "the Parthenon," "the Cathedrale de Chartres," "Aeneas," "ballet and opera," and thereby works to deconstruct the kind of European myth that served as subtext for Joyce and Eliot. In these poems the subtext acts as metaphor rather than irony; in the case of Marlatt's use of the Winter Ceremonial, the subtext enlarges the vision of the poem temporally and culturally. It enlarges it sociologically in Kroetsch's *Seed Catalogue*, Bowering's *Baseball*, and Ondaatje's story of Billy the Kid.

•

"I'm asking myself what holds me here / and how did I get here / treading air in an interval," Stuart McKinnon tells us in *The Intervals*. This is another kind of metaphor, another way of showing wholeness in the absence of plot: the recurrent image— here the interval, interval of time, *inter vallum*, narrow physical spaces of McKinnon's poem. In a note to his long poem *Image-nations*, Robin Blaser tells the reader to "read by image" or else "be stopped by...a misreading of the one here that is flowing in every direction." The image that is one and many, that brings the poem to wholeness by flowing in every direction: this is the sea image in Dudek's *Europe*, an image-rhyme that grows into central metaphor; it is the pervasively metaphoric rings of Marlatt's *Rings*; it is the dominant focussing sign, nakedness, that is reflected ultimately in the stripped-down language of Phyllis Webb's *Naked Poems*. These poems require a reading which is not a relating of text and subtext, not a construing of narrative sequence, but an identifying and interrelating of the recurring elements.

•

One of the recurring metaphors of recent Canadian long poems is the autobiography of the writer. The sequence of life-events enters the poem, not to become one of its subjects, as it does in Wordsworth's *Excursion*, but to occasion its images, and to provide some framework for its language. Life-structure here becomes poem-structure; life-event becomes recurring image. We see this non-plot use of autobiography in such disparate poems as Norris' *Autokinesis*, McKinnon's *The Intervals*, Bowering's *Autobiology* and *At War with the U.S.*, Dudek's *En Mexico*, and particularly in life-long poems such as *Continuation*, *Field Notes*, and *The Martyrology*. When Marlatt expands *Rings* into *What Matters*, the life-metaphor is given new emphasis by the inclusion of journal entries. Again we see the impulse not to delay but to prolong, to have the poem not be about time but in it, not to be about the life but within it.

Correspondingly, the voice of these poems tends to be oral and personal. The texts are transcripts of spoken words. The voice is specific; to engage such a poem is to engage an actual historical consciousness—the long lines of Nichol's *The Martyrology*, the increasingly halting lines of Webb's *Naked Poems*, the forced ebullience of Kroetsch's *The Sad Phoenician*, the ironic antitheses of Atwood's *Power Politics*, the tentative, groping syntax of Marlatt's *Steveston* and *Vancouver Poems*, the balanced considerations of Dudek's *Atlantis*. In Dudek and Marlatt particularly, the voice is exploratory; syntactic changes in mid-sentence denote not only an attentive curiosity of mind but a poem of which the shape only becomes known to the writer word by word, a poem which is being written simultaneously to being lived. These changes reflect that the life-process of discovering the shape of the poem is a part of that poem's shape, and must, therefore, be preserved. The process of writing is paradoxically here part of the goal of writing.

In all cases it is also notable that the life-metaphor is cast in non-romantic, low-mimetic terms—a sharp contrast to highly enhanced life-portraits which act as metaphors in the long poems of U.S. poets such as Olson or Duncan. Yet the tone of such Canadian poems is still closer to celebration than to irony. In my reading of them, their use of an ordinary, non-romantic vocabulary to present the life-experience argues that the ordinary itself is remarkable, that there is magic in a slow walk through McKinnon's Kingston or, in Fred Wah's case, in the drawing of the daily breath; that the life-experience does not need the enhancement of rhetoric to reveal its richness. As in my reading of the impulse to prolong, I read these signs as ones of affirmation, celebration.

Related to the undramatized voice of these poems is their implied rejection of Robert Duncan's sense of the serial poem as a poem in which the images are dictated by an "Other" world and in which the act of writing is analogous to the transubstantiation of the Host. Any similarity to the American serial poem is to Spicer's sense of a poem in which the poet is "in relationship" to an "outside"; in the Canadian poem the outside is psychologically or phenomenally present—there is none of the possibility of angels or Martians which Spicer at least half-seriously held open. The outside can be a journey or a place in Dudek, human relationship in Marlatt, the personal unconscious in Nichol's *Martyrology* and Bowering's *Autobiology*, a subtext of story or image in numerous others. In the Canadian long poem there is no implied division between the actual and the real; the actual is the real; the phenomenal is the noumenal and can explode, like Billy the Kid's revolver, with magic. So it is Spicer's voice that is closest to the voices we hear in these poems; the language of the street, in Kroetsch, Bowering, McKay, Kiyooka, Ondaatje, can abruptly speak as the language of the holy.

•

A peculiarity of the recent Canadian long poem has been the large number of poems built around a metaphoric strategy, a pre-selected image which simultaneously defines the area of the poem and provides a field of potential recurrence on which the prolongation of the poem will depend. Often the poem develops as a series of responses to these chosen images, as Nichol's current suite of prose-poems, "Organ Music," responds to various body-organs, or Bowering's *Curious* responded to his experiences of various North American writers. Often the subtext is used in this way, not as a counterpoint to the main text as in Atwood's *Susanna Moodie*, but as a set of images to which the main text will react. This is Bowering's use of the subtext of the Geneva Tarot pack in *Genève*, Kroetsch's use of his seed catalogue. The subtext here is a provocation, a stimulus, a key that may unlock unanticipated material within the writer. Many of these sets of images are theoretically unlimited in potential, particularly if the writer responds at random to their content, as Kroetsch appears to do with his *Seed Catalogue*. A systematic approach, however, can create a numerically limited possibility; in Bowering's *Genève* the poem cannot proceed beyond the thirty-eight Tarot cards the poet has selected as its occasion. The open territory of such a poem is a kind of inner space, within numeric parameters, within its images, within the text of each section of the poem. There is a strong flavour of challenge about many of these strategies, as if the poet were challenging the metaphor to reveal meaning. In *Europe*, Dudek begins his voyage by instructing himself to "Let it speak." Marlatt similarly begins her responses to *Steveston*: "Imagine a town." By these strategies the poet appears to limit his poem so that it may grow, to concentrate on a metaphor so that its largest potential can be realized, to select the small so that it may be long. Each one of these poems is reminiscent of the eighteenth-century English poet William Cowper's long poem *The Task*, begun at a patron's suggestion that he resolve his difficulties with content by focussing simply on his sofa, and on the events it witnessed. To set oneself a task: that a Mexican journey—*En Mexico, Sitting in Mexico, Zócalo*—become a poem, that an object—Kroetsch's lemon, Kiyooka's gloves, Bowering's baseball, Wah's and Suknaski's mountains—reveal more than the poet can anticipate.

•

To see more than can be anticipated. To be surprised. When surprises cease, the poem ends, or should end. Many long poems are not terminated but abandoned, like my poem "The Mirror," when an ending is recognized in the cessation of surprise. Some poets speak of relief in having ended as if the demands of surprise were as exhausting as those of some life-threatening emergency or high-risk sport. In our time these surprises are no longer just ones of plot but surprises of image, of diction, surprises of phrase, of linguistic and metaphoric event. And not frivolous surprise. In the contemporary long poem when the poet surprises one, or when he jests, he is paradoxically at his most serious. In the traditional narrative—I think here of Pratt's oatmeal metaphor for the Scotsmen of *Toward the Last Spike*—the jest indicated that the poet was being genial, less than fully serious.

"Aw narrative/is a telling blow." The jest can be a quick one-liner, as Bowering here in *Allophanes*; it can be an extended anecdote as Kroetsch's tale of Al Purdy's Caribou horse galloping through the Chateau Lacombe restaurant. In Don McKay's *Long Sault* the rapids reappear as an itinerant saxophonist in a Kapuskasing bar; in Atwood's *Power Politics* the narrator's lover keeps metamorphosizing into commercial images; in Nichol's *The True Eventual Story of Billy the Kid*, Billy dies when "he snuck up on himself and shot himself from behind the grocery store." The highest truth here is metaphorical truth. Like Billy, truth sneaks up behind us in the long poem as surprise image or absurd pun. When surprises cease, the poem ends, truth ends.

•

Bowering again in *Allophanes:*

> Have a seat on my language,
> & here we go,
>
> lecherously, thru the flowing world
> of Hera's clitoris.
>
> With a neo classical
> Neal Cassady, what a driver!
>
> . . . .
>
> Drive right past that lady, that's
> St As Is.

To me this is the central task of the long poem: to drive right past St As Is into new territory, into new languages, into surprise. To write long poems that are not, in sign, in image, in structure, like earlier long poems. To create, or steal, or by stealing create, new signs out of the languages of other forms—as the collage was stolen from the visual arts, as radio play was transformed into long poem by Birney in *Trial of a City*, as Gertrude Stein's syntax is taken into the long poem by Nichol in *The True Eventual Story* and by Bowering in *Autobiology*, as the language of the playscript is taken into the long poem by Coleman in *Some Plays: on Words*. In very recent times the long poem has begun to encroach on the novel, so that we have long poems, like Nichol's *True Eventual Story* again, which were intended as prose, and long poems, like Ondaatje's *The Man with Seven Toes* and *The Collected Works of Billy the Kid*, or Marlatt's *What Matters*, that resemble novels. And in Marlatt, Bowering, Ondaatje, Nichol, we have writers whose prose works are in many respects indistinguishable from their long poems, and can be read—as Kroetsch reads Marlatt's *Zócalo*—as long poems. I expect the long poem to encroach further upon fiction—not only on the prose measure, character-relationships, and satire— but on the viewpoint shifts and the jesting hypothetical incidents that have marked the recent fiction of Sukenick, Barthelme, and Fowles. And to encroach elsewhere. For the successful long poem exults in new signs, thefts, adventure.

•

I have been speaking of the Canadian long poem, yet almost half the poems I have cited are British Columbia long poems. The long poem in British Columbia occupies a much larger role in poetry than it does elsewhere in Canada, although it is firmly connected to major work by non-B.C. writers like Ondaatje, Kroetsch, McKay, Dudek, and Atwood. The principal work of most of its major poets—Birney, Livesay, Webb, Bowering, Nichol, Marlatt, Blaser—has been in the long poem. B.C. poets as a group tend away from the occasional, place-independent poem of the cosmopolitan literary periodical and toward extended work which is frequently shaped by larger circumstance and which requires at least in part the metaphor of the ongoing life. This longer poem is characterized by a specific sense of the poet's relationship to his world and society; rather than seeing himself as solitary, independent, and in an adversarial relationship to others, a common view in the Canadian lyric, this writer of the long poem sees himself as working in a collaborative relationship with person and event—relying partially, as I have suggested, on 'surprise' and discovery from 'outside' the poet's conscious self for the growth and movement of his poem. The dominance of the long poem in B.C. poetry reflects a different view of nature from the basically apprehensive one of central Canada and a differently weighted conception of human and literary possibility.

The long poem, one might say, is the form that B.C. poets enter when they choose to take on the role of poet with especial seriousness—to begin a long-term cooperation with language and event, to engage time, to take on history, space and process in an attitude of adventure, risk, and play and in something resembling life-size scale. This fact lures one to make hypotheses: a portrait of British Columbians as adventurers of the imagination, a history of B.C. long poems beginning in the log-books of Cook, Meares, Vancouver, an environment sufficiently supportive of human life that it inspires trust in other large natural structures, particularly language and metaphor. Or perhaps a geography that actively contextualizes the individual life with landmarks that extend in space (as in land and sea forms) or time (as in plant life or river flow); a geography that depicts the self as part of something vaster and more hopeful than itself, something which grows and surprises, like a long poem.